Chambers
English
Grammar

D1418803

Chambers English Grammar
A. J. Taylor BA has over 35 years' experience teaching English, French and the classics. He also has experience as an Assistant Examiner for the Oxford & Cambridge Schools Examination Board.

Chambers
English
Grammar

A. J. Taylor

Chambers

Published 1990 by W & R Chambers Ltd,
43–45 Annandale Street, Edinburgh EH7 4AZ

British Library Cataloguing in Publication Data
Taylor, A. J.
    Chambers pocket guide to English grammar.
    1. English language. Grammar
    I. Title
    428.2

ISBN 0-550-18034-6

Acknowledgment
I am grateful to my wife and family for their constant help
and encouragement, and to my pupils for all they have
taught me.

Typeset by Pillans & Wilson Specialist Litho Printers Ltd,
Edinburgh
Printed in Singapore by Chong Moh Offset Printing Pte Ltd

Contents

Introduction

The Advantage of English Grammar

Older pupils at school and students of all ages will find this book useful: it will help them to understand better the structure of the English language, and will explain many of the difficulties they meet in applying their knowledge of their own language to the study of a foreign language. Parents and teachers, too, will be enabled to refresh their own understanding of grammatical ideas and terms when they need to explain them to their children. Finally, all those who wish to use English 'correctly' and confidently in their social and business lives will find here the answers to their questions.

English Grammar in the Twentieth Century

From the mid-twentieth century onwards English grammar has fallen out of favour. During the educational ferment and enthusiasm of the post-war world, it was easily labelled old-fashioned, dull, restrictive and therefore unnecessary. As the result, the teaching of traditional grammar in our schools declined. Pupils (said a new orthodoxy) must by every means be encouraged to develop their powers of creative self-expression; their language abilities would take care of themselves, and time spent on English grammar would be valuable time wasted.

This development was understandable, and in some ways even desirable. In the late nineteenth and early twentieth centuries, grammar teaching *was* by all accounts often dull and dogmatic; the grammar of the classical languages was applied in all its rigorous detail directly to modern languages; it could be uninspiring and restrictive for the majority of pupils. To many boys and girls of those days reading and writing could well appear to be a hunt-the-split-infinitive extension of the grammar lesson.

However, in some ways the remedy has proved worse than the disease. The resultant hostility to grammar has meant that several generations of pupils have passed through our schools without gaining any knowledge of the language substructure that was once acquired at an early stage. Pupils themselves – as they, their teachers and their parents are now beginning to suspect – are the losers when this happens. Employers prefer employees who can express themselves in reasonably grammatical English. University and other advanced students need to express themselves accurately in the course of their studies. At school or university alike, students of foreign languages need grammatical understanding to deal with the more advanced work or to acquire a new language at speed; for in learning languages there is a useful 'carry over' process between the structure of one language and that of another. All this comes at a time when we are increasingly involved with the languages of other Europeans, who still learn and understand the basics of traditional grammar.

English Grammar – Practical Requirements for Today

This book is based on the following beliefs:

First, modern English grammar must enable us to identify the *functions of words*. Many words in our language have a variety of different uses, which need to be recognized and described. Only when we can see what part a word is playing in a particular phrase or sentence can we say confidently, 'This word is a noun or adjective or. . .' In this respect, English is far more flexible than the ancient languages and than many modern ones; for instance, a *table* names something and is a noun, *table*-tennis uses the same word as an adjective, and to '*table* an amendment' uses it as a verb.

Second, the grammar of modern English, like the grammars of French, German, Italian, Spanish and the ancient classical languages, is about the *relationship between words*. 'The *table* collapsed', 'I am polishing the *table*', 'I am giving the *table* a polish', 'The *table's* surface is scratched', 'Put the plate on the *table*' – all these illustrate different relationships between the noun *table* and the other words it is used with.

Third, *grammatical terms* are a convenient way of labelling and referring to the functions of words and their relationships. The simple grammatical terminology used, and explained, in this book will be easily grasped in a world where 'psychosomatic' and 'polyunsaturated' are readily accepted, and where the younger generation can explain the mysteries of computer language to their parents and grandparents.

The Contents of This Book
The book provides a simple introduction to the 'nuts and bolts' of traditional English grammar. It is intended for those who never learned any grammar, as well as for those who have forgotten what they once knew.

It explains the division of words into eight *parts of speech*, emphasizing the importance of the *function* of words in making the division. A chapter is devoted to each part of speech, which is defined and illustrated. The *traditional grammatical terms* are introduced and explained. In the first place, this is because they are still familiar (if only vaguely) to many readers of a book like this, while modern attempts to replace them have gained little following outside academic circles. Moreover, the traditional terms have a currency beyond *English* grammar; the student of foreign languages will still encounter them, particularly in advanced studies here or abroad. A further advantage is that they make possible a more intelligent use of English and foreign dictionaries; the list of abbreviations at the front of a dictionary may reveal that *v.t.* means 'verb transitive', but what if neither 'verb' nor 'transitive' means anything to the reader? Finally, as I have already said, these grammatical terms are a convenience; it is so much easier to say 'the object of the verb' or 'the accusative case after the verb' than 'the word naming the thing or person that the action word does something to'. (Readers of this book may choose between 'object' and 'accusative'; they will find both here.)

At various stages the structure of short sentences is analysed to highlight the *relationship* between words in speech and writing. Later chapters examine the function of *word-groups* (phrases and clauses) as expanded forms of individual parts of speech, and this is illustrated by the analysis of a complex sentence into its component parts. A final chapter is devoted to capital letters and punctuation.

There is a detailed index, so that the book may be used for reference. There is also a short personal selection of books I have found helpful.

A.J.T.

1

Kinds of Words

This book is about words and how we use them.

We speak, read and hear many hundreds of words every day of our lives; and thousands more are to be found in dictionaries and other books. If we are to have some mastery of words, rather than being overwhelmed by their sheer number, we must borrow the method the Romans used for governing the peoples of their empire: divide and rule.

All words may be divided into eight kinds according to *how we use them*. The eight kinds are called the *eight parts of speech*. Here they are:

NOUNS	are the names of people or things – eg, John, house, nation, anxiety. (*Noun* is the English form of the Latin word for a *name*.)
PRONOUNS	are used *instead of nouns* to mention people or things without naming them – eg, he, it, they. (In Latin, *pro-* means *instead of*.)
ADJECTIVES	describe nouns and pronouns – eg, little, white, foreign. (In Latin, *ad-* means *to*; *adjective* comes from the Latin word for something *added to* a noun or pronoun.)
VERBS	are actions – eg, hear, went, laughed. As we shall see later, there are also a few verbs like *is, were* and *becomes* which need another word to

complete their meanings. (*Verb* comes from the Latin *verbum* which means a *word* – so called because a verb is the keyword in a sentence.)

ADVERBS

describe and are attached *to* verbs in particular, as their name suggests; but they can also be attached to other parts of speech except nouns and pronouns. What adjectives do for nouns and pronouns is done for all other parts of speech by adverbs. To a verb, for instance, adverbs can contribute information about when, where and how the action happened – eg, '*Yesterday* our team played a match *there successfully.*' *Yesterday*, *there* and *successfully* are all adverbs which give information about the action of the verb *played*.

CONJUNCTIONS

join words (eg, cat *and* mouse) and join sentences (eg, We admire him *because* he is kind). The word conjunction means *joining together*. (*Con* is the Latin for *together*, and *junction* is from the Latin verb meaning *join*.)

PREPOSITIONS

are words whose *position* is in front of nouns and pronouns. Most prepositions have to do with *place* – eg, *on* the table, *in* the newspaper, *from* London; or with *time* – eg, *after* tea, *before* the war, *during* the lecture. (*Pre* is the Latin for *in front of*.)

INTERJECTIONS

are exclamations. Their name means that they are *thrown among* the other words in conversation or (less frequently) in writing. The polite ones of previous generations include *Good heavens!*, *By Jove!* and

2

Good Gracious!. Alas!, many interjections both ancient and modern are not considered polite.

These are the eight kinds of words, known as the *parts of speech*. The following chapters examine and illustrate each part of speech in greater detail. First, however, two cautions are necessary.

1. *In order to be certain what part of speech a word is, we must always look at its function.* Words are divided into eight kinds according to how we use them. Remember that many words have several different uses. Furthermore, words are alive, and old words are continually acquiring new uses. It is important always to ask how a word is being used in a given sentence, as the examples below make clear.

   a) The ship struck a *rock*: *rock* names something, and is therefore a noun.
   b) They enjoy *rock* music: *rock* describes the noun music, and is therefore an adjective.
   c) Don't *rock* the boat: *rock* is an action, and is therefore a verb.

2. *Some words perform two functions at the same time.* Chapter 5 contains the relative pronoun, which is both conjunction and pronoun; Chapter 13 contains the conjunctive adverb, which combines the jobs of conjunction and adverb.

Summary of the Eight Parts of Speech
   1. Nouns
   2. Pronouns
   3. Adjectives
   4. Verbs
   5. Adverbs
   6. Conjunctions
   7. Prepositions
   8. Interjections

2
Nouns – The Four Types

Definition

What's in a name? Or, since nouns are the names of people and things, what's in a noun? The answer is that *in* a noun is the *meaning* which it brings to us when we hear it or read it.

The meaning may take the form of a picture, an idea or a feeling – or a mixture of all three. It may be a particular meaning, conveyed by words such as *London* or *Sherlock Holmes*; on the other hand, words like *city* or *detective* contain a very general meaning. Those with a particular meaning are proper nouns; those with a general meaning are common nouns.

Besides these, there are two other types of nouns: collective nouns, which name collections of people or things; and abstract nouns, which refer to 'abstractions' that cannot be perceived by our senses.

Proper Nouns

These name particular people or things, like *John Smith* and *France*. They are called proper names and they begin with capital letters. When we say 'I saw *John Smith* this afternoon', we mean a particular person called *John Smith*; if somebody says 'I went to *France* via *Dover* and *Calais*', he is speaking of a particular country and also mentioning two particular towns. Similarly, *Scrooge* in *A Christmas Carol* by Charles Dickens and *Professor Moriarty* in the Sherlock Holmes stories are the proper names of particular characters in fiction.

Sometimes nouns which were originally the proper names of particular people are given a more general meaning. For instance, Scrooge becomes a picturesque way of saying 'a miser' ('They're real Scrooges, never give anything to anybody if they can help it!'). Here the noun *Scrooge* no longer names a particular character but is being used like the common nouns in the next section.

Common Nouns

These name people or things of which there may be many of the same kind, like *citizen* and *country*. Millions of people share the name of *citizen*; and there are hundreds of geographical areas, each of which may be called a *country*. These words are called common nouns because, like common land, they are not private property.

Collective Nouns

These name collections of people or things – eg, *family*, *committee, flock, herd, school,* and *trade union*. Each of these is a single unit though it contains a collection of members, which is why it is often given a singular verb: 'A committee *was* elected' (rather than *were*). 'The trade union *has* supported this policy' (rather than *have*). But a plural verb is more suitable when we are thinking about the individuals in a group rather than about the behaviour of the group as a unit: 'The committee *have* been arguing all the morning and *are* unable to reach agreement' (rather than *has* and *is*).

Whether we use a singular or a plural verb in sentences like these, we must be careful when it is followed by a pronoun (it, its, they, them, their):

'The committee *was* elected and held *its* (not *their*) first meeting.'

'The committee *are* unable to agree about *their* (not *its*) policy.'

Abstract Nouns

Each of the three types of nouns which we have met so far names people or things which can be seen, heard, touched, smelt or tasted. In other words we are aware of them through one or more of the five senses. Abstract nouns, however, name qualities, states and actions which *on their own* cannot be perceived by our senses: we can see them, hear them, etc, only in the people or things to which they belong.

The quality called *beauty*, for instance, may belong to a scene or a person, and we use the adjective *beautiful* (full of beauty) in speaking of them. We can see beauty in a beautiful scene or a beautiful woman, but we cannot see beauty on its own when it is taken away (*abstracted*) from them. Hence the *names of qualities* like beauty, ugliness, loudness, hardness and strength are called abstract nouns.

Similarly, a baby is in a state called *infancy*; many people live in a state called *poverty*; and sometimes people may be in a state called *terror* ('in a terrified state', we say) or *happiness*. We can see, hear and touch children in infancy, people in poverty, and people in states of terror or happiness; but we cannot see these states of infancy, poverty, terror or happiness when they are taken away (*abstracted*) from the people or things they belong to. Hence the *names of states* like these are called abstract nouns.

The same is true of a noun which names an action. Many nouns ending in *-ing* come into this category. You cannot see an action called *jumping* or *reading* unless someone is doing it. These and other *names of actions* are abstract nouns.

Summary of the Types of Nouns

1.	Proper nouns	Proper names.
2.	Common nouns	Common to a number of people or things at the same time.
3.	Collective nouns	Collections of people or things, each collection being regarded as a single unit.
4.	Abstract nouns	naming a *quality* belonging to someone/thing; or a *state* someone/thing is in; or an *action* someone/thing does.

3

Nouns – Number and Gender

Number
This is a convenient technical term with an obvious meaning. What number is a word? means is this word singular or plural? Most languages alter or add to the endings of nouns to make them plural; in English -*s* is added to most nouns, but there are many exceptions, which we learn by trial and error and by consulting a dictionary.

Gender
This is a topic which has little importance for those who are concerned only with *English* grammar. However, you may find a brief explanation helpful if you are meeting a foreign language for the first time.

The direct common ancestor of a number of European languages, including those of France, Italy and Spain, was Latin; hence these languages are called *Romance* languages because they are derived from the language spoken by the Romans. In Latin each noun and pronoun was thought of as being a masculine word *or* a feminine word *or* a neuter word (*neuter* simply meaning *neither* – ie, neither masculine nor feminine). These are called the three genders.

Nouns used for males (human and animal) were naturally masculine, and similarly nouns used for females were feminine; but the names of things were masculine or feminine or neuter nouns, for no immediately obvious reason in many cases. 'Head', for example, was neuter, but 'hand' was feminine and 'foot' and 'eye' were masculine.

Latin spread through Italy and the rest of Roman-occupied Europe as a spoken (as well as an official written) language; and gradually this spoken language developed in different countries into what we call the Romance languages. On the way it underwent many changes. One early casualty was the neuter gender. So French, Italian and Spanish developed with two genders only, masculine and feminine. On the other hand German, which is not a Romance language, still has three genders.

What has survived in these languages from the Latin way of thought is the rule that an adjective must show that it belongs to its noun by having a masculine or feminine *ending* as the case may be. The Frenchman will wish you *Bon jour* (Good day) using the masculine ending of the adjective meaning 'good' because *jour* is a masculine noun; but he will wish you *Bonne chance* (Good luck) using the feminine ending because *chance* is feminine.

Those who learn English are spared the whole business of gender. But it is an essential concept when you are learning almost any other language.

Summary of Number and Gender in Nouns

1. The number of a noun is either singular or plural.
2. The three genders are masculine, feminine and neuter. The idea of gender in nouns is of no practical importance in English but is essential in the study of other languages.

4

Nouns – The Cases: Sentences I

To decide which part of speech a word is, we must always look at how it is used – at its function within a sentence. Similarly, to decide which *case* a noun is, we must look at how the noun is used in a particular context.

The ways in which nouns are used in speaking and writing are technically called their *cases*. The names of the various cases were originally Latin labels invented for easy reference. (Just as today every modern scientific development produces its own new names or collections of initials for exactly the same purpose.)

In Latin, nouns used in different ways were given different *case-endings*, something which in modern English occurs only in the possessive forms (eg, brother*'s* and brother*s'*). Nouns in the modern Romance languages have no case-endings, but there are some in German nouns. Pronouns, however, in all these languages including our own do have various different forms according to their cases (see Chapter 5). In some ancient languages, groups of case-endings were organized into *declensions*. The word *declension* is explained at the end of this chapter.

The old *case names* derived from Latin are less used in English grammar today. However, they are still a handy way of referring to cases. The five ways of using nouns, each with its technical case name, are outlined below.

Nominative Case (Subject and Complement)
The word nominative is connected with *nominate=give a name to*. It gives a name to the main actor or subject of interest in a sentence.

1. *The noun or pronoun which is the subject* of the sentence is said to be in the nominative case.

   That *author* (subject) has published another novel.

   We (subject) shall buy a copy.

2. *Any other noun or pronoun which is identified with the subject* is also in the nominative case.

   This *valley* (subject), now a beautiful *sight*, was once a *battlefield*.

Besides the subject *valley* there are two other nominative nouns in this sentence: *sight*, which enlarges or fills out the subject; and *battlefield*, which is linked to the subject by the verb *was* and gives us more information about the subject.

A few verbs, like *is* and *was*, are often followed by a nominative like *battlefield*; it *completes* their sense and is called a *complement*. (See Chapter 7 for a fuller explanation.)

Vocative Case (Person Spoken To)

This is the *calling* case (a vocation, of course, still means a calling). It is used for the person or thing spoken to. In old English and poetry it is often preceded by 'O' (not 'Oh', which is an exclamation).

In written English the vocative has to be separated from the rest of the sentence by a sensible comma; otherwise confusion may result. A schoolmaster, seeing a pupil busily cutting his name on his desk, might ask him: 'Why are you damaging that, *boy*?' Omit the comma before the vocative, representing the slight pause in the spoken sentence, and the meaning will appear very different.

This case is occasionally called the 'nominative of address', but vocative is just as easy to understand and has the advantage of being shorter.

The vocatives are italicized in the examples below:

'*Friends, Romans, Countrymen,* lend me your ears.' (Shakespeare, *Julius Caesar*)

Now, *reader*, do you understand the vocative case?

Accusative Case (Object)

The name of this case has a legal background. Since the accused person in a court of law was the *object* of a charge against him, accusative came to be applied in grammar to

1. *A noun or pronoun which was the object of (or at the receiving end of) the action of a verb.*

   'When a dog bites a *man*, that is not news, but when a man bites a *dog*, that is news.'

(Note that the objects of a verb – *man* and *dog* in this example – are called *direct objects*. This is to distinguish them from *indirect objects*, which are explained in the section on the *Dative Case*.)

The use of the accusative for the object of a verb was extended to include

2. *A noun or pronoun following a preposition and regarded as the object of the preposition.*

   On the *table*; from *London*; after *tea*.

The three nouns – table, London and tea – are objects of the prepositions and therefore said to be in the accusative case.

Dative Case (Indirect Object)
This gains its name from the Latin verb meaning 'to give', from which is also derived the word *data* – the *given* facts on which a theory may be built. Because of the origin of its name, the dative is sometimes described as the giving case. It is more correctly described as the case of the recipient – *the person (or thing) to whom something is given or for whom something is done*. A shorter way of putting this is to say that the dative is the case of the *indirect object* of an action.

I gave *John* a book.

I bought *John* a present.

You will realize from the previous section on the accusative case that the direct object of the action of the verb *gave* is *book*, and the direct object of the verb *bought* is *present*.

The word *John* in each sentence acts as a kind of secondary object of the verbs. *John* is the *indirect object* in the dative case. This becomes clearer if we rewrite the two examples in their alternative English form (notice the change of word order).

I gave a *book* (direct object) *to John* (indirect object).

I bought a *present* (direct object) *for John* (indirect object). In these rewritten sentences the dative phrases *to John* and *for John* replace the one-word dative *John* and make its case quite clear. Only when these to/for forms are used is the indirect object (dative) clearly distinguished in English from the direct object (accusative).

This is often a source of difficulty in the early stages of learning foreign languages; when object pronouns replace the nouns, the distinction between the two objects is particularly important to the student of another language. Each of the following examples contains an indirect object and a direct object; the alternative to/for form is given in brackets.

I am offering *you* a job. (I am offering a job *to you*.)

Please pass *me* the salt. (Please pass the salt *to me*.)

He handed *every shopper* a leaflet. (He handed a leaflet *to every shopper*.)

What an interesting letter you wrote *me*! (What an interesting letter you wrote *to me*!)

Has she told *her sister* this story? (Has she told this story *to her sister*?)

Genitive Case (Possessor)

The name is derived from a whole range of Latin words which have to do with the reproduction of the species by humans, animals and plants. Hence the English word 'progenitors', meaning ancestors, and the Italian *genitori* for parents. It is not difficult to see how the idea of belonging to, or being the possession of, a family or species arose from this. So the genitive is the *possessive case*.

In modern English it is only in the genitive that nouns still have case endings (*'s* and *s'*). The genitive case is also expressed by the word *of* in front of a noun or pronoun.

The genitive case of pronouns is dealt with in Chapter 5. The genitive case of nouns can be summarized in a rule with certain exceptions.

RULE: *The train's destination* is equivalent to *the destination of the train* (singular), and *the trains' destination* is equivalent to *the destination of the trains* (plural).

EXCEPTIONS:

1. Plural words which do not end in *s* are treated like the singular *train's* in the first example, as in *men's, women's* and *children's*.

2. Singular words which already end in *s* may be treated in two ways.

   '*James's* house' is as correct as '*James'* house'. You will be in respectable company whichever you write. However, the first alternative (*James's*) is generally preferred today; it follows the old advice to write the *'s* in the possessive form of names like this if it is pronounced. On this principle we should write *St James's Park* and *Prince Charles's wedding* because the *'s* is pronounced.

3. Singular nouns ending in *-nce* form their possessives without the apostrophe *s*, as in 'for *convenience'* sake'. Here again pronunciation is a safe guide.

Declension

This word is not used in English grammar, but an explanation will help those who meet it for the first time in the study of a foreign language. Declension (which is linked to the verb 'decline') means 'going down a slope'. Ancient teachers, who wished their pupils to have a picture of the noun's case-endings, taught them to regard the nominative, the case of the subject, as the 'top' case; the other, less important cases were thought of as being at various stages down the slope from the top. The order of the cases on the slope varied, perhaps with different teachers. In other words the idea of a declension was used as a kind of early visual aid.

The next stage was to divide the nouns of a language into groups according to the different types of case-endings they possessed. The groups were called the first declension of nouns, the second declension, and so on. Classical Greek had three declensions and Latin had five.

This grouping of nouns was important in the study of any language which had a variety of case-endings; but it is unnecessary in English, which has hardly any.

Sentences I: Subject and Predicate

In this chapter we have considered the various ways in which we use nouns (and *pro*nouns) to convey our meaning to other people. The fullest meaning is expressed when we combine these words with others in groups called sentences. Very young children use nouns to name the people and things in their surroundings: Mummy, story, tea. In time they combine these nouns with other words: 'Mummy read story', and later 'Mummy read story after tea' (*read* being at this stage either a request or a statement). They are beginning to speak in the groups of words we call sentences.

Each sentence contains two parts:
1. *The subject* (in the nominative case) names the person(s) or thing(s) the sentence is speaking about.
2. *The predicate* says something about the subject. The essential word in the predicate is the *verb*.

In each of the first three examples that follow, the subject stands first, immediately before the verb of the predicate. This is sometimes called the normal position of the subject in a sentence. In the third sentence notice how the subject noun *valley* is filled out by a further group of words (*now. . .sight*), which themselves form part of the subject.

Subject	Predicate
1. Birds	sing
2. Jack and Jill	went up the hill
3. This valley, now a beautiful sight,	was once a battlefield

In sentences of the following two kinds the subject is usually not in the 'normal' place:

Questions reverse the subject and part of the verb (you may have met something similar in French or German). For example: *Have you heard the birds singing?*

Exclamations place the exclamatory words first, whether they form part of the subject or not. For example: *What wonderful stories the old soldier told!*

If you are in doubt about the subjects and predicates of these sentences, pick out first the verbs (*have heard; told*), then the subjects (*you; the old soldier*). You should then be able to arrange the subjects and the predicates in the following way:

	Subject	Predicate
4.	you	have heard the birds singing
5.	the old soldier	told what wonderful stories

Finally, there are sentences which in modern English do not appear to have a subject. These are:

Commands or requests – eg, *Listen carefully*. Here the subject is always *you*, and it is understood although it is not expressed. However, in old English and in modern colloquial speech we find: Choose *you* this day whom you will serve (1611 version of the Bible).

Listen *you*! *You* listen carefully!

In all of these instances of commands, the subject is *you* and the rest of the sentence forms the predicate.

A sentence begins with a capital letter and ends with a full stop; a question mark or an exclamation mark replaces the full stop at the end of a question or an exclamation.

Later chapters will deal in more detail with the division of sentences into subjects and predicates, and with the various stops used in writing sentences.

Summary

1. The cases are:

Nominative	The subject and the complement
Vocative	The person spoken to
Accusative	The object of a verb or of a preposition
Dative	The indirect object – often expressed by *to* or *for*
Genitive	The possessor – often expressed by *of*

(Note: In Latin two more case names were used, the ablative and the locative; these have no place in English or in other modern languages.)

2. Sentences are groups of nouns and other words which convey our meaning. A sentence consists of two parts: a *subject* and a *predicate* (which includes the verb of the sentence).

5

Pronouns

Definition
Pronouns are used instead of nouns to mention people or things without naming them. In other words, they are substitutes for nouns.

Types of Pronoun
This chapter deals with five groups of pronouns:

1. Personal pronouns
2. Relative pronouns
3. Interrogative pronouns
4. Demonstrative pronouns
5. Other pronouns

The pronouns of the first three types possess several different forms according to their cases.

Personal Pronouns
These are easily recognized and seen to be acting as substitutes for nouns. Any speaker or writer uses 'I' to mean himself as the subject of the sentence; this word is described as the *first person singular* pronoun, representing the first or most important person in the speaker's experience. He calls the person he is speaking to 'you' (in earlier English, 'thou'), and this word is naturally called the *second person singular*. He speaks about someone (or something) else, whom he may describe as 'he', 'she' or 'it': these words represent the *third person singular*. (You'll notice from 'it' that *person* as a grammatical term includes things and well as people.)

The plural equivalents of these singular pronouns are 'we' (*first person plural*), 'you'(*second person plural*) and 'they' (*third person plural*).

All these personal pronouns so far are in the nominative case (see Chapter 4). The Table of Personal Pronouns shows how the forms of pronouns change in other cases. Archaic forms are given in brackets.

Table of Personal Pronouns

	Nominative (Subject)	Accusative (Object)	Dative (Indirect Object)	Genitive (Possessive)	
				(1)	(2)
SINGULAR					
First Person	I	me	me	my	mine
Second Person	you (thou)	you (thee)	you (thee)	your (thy)	yours (thine)
Third Person	he	him	him	his	his
	she	her	her	her	hers
	it	it	it	its	its
	one	one	one	one's	one's
PLURAL					
First Person	we	us	us	our	ours
Second Person	you (ye)	you	you	your	yours
Third Person	they	them	them	their	theirs

Here are some points arising from the Table of Personal Pronouns. Please refer to the table as you read them.

You, your, yours were originally second person plural pronouns, but we now use them as the normal singular forms as well. A similar process has taken place in other European languages, where, however, the old singular forms equivalent to *thou* are still in everyday use in the family and between friends.

Accusative and dative cases have the same forms, and they are distinguishable only by the way they are used. The same is true of nouns, as we have discovered in Chapter 4. To illustrate this, here are sentences using the pronoun *us* in the two different ways:

1. 'Our friends invited *us* to a party.' *Us* is the direct object (accusative) of the verb *invited*.

2. 'Our friends gave *us* birthday presents.' *Us* is equivalent to *to us*; it is therefore the indirect object (dative).

Genitives are printed in two columns in the table. Most personal pronouns have different possessive forms in the two columns, eg (1) *my*, (2) *mine*; but *his*, *its* and *one's* have the same forms in each column. The two columns correspond to two different uses of these possessive or genitive forms.

(1) are the forms used in front of nouns, exactly like adjectives – eg, *my* house; *his* room; *your* uncle; *their* friends. In other languages you will often find these forms called possessive adjectives.
(2) are the forms used *instead of* nouns – eg:
This room is *mine* (= *my room*);
I like my room; I do not like *yours* (= *your room*);
We prefer our friends to *theirs* (= *their friends*).

Notice that *yours, hers, its, ours, theirs,* unlike the genitive cases of nouns, never have an apostrophe (') before the *s*. (*It's* always stands for *it is*.)

In sixteenth- and seventeenth-century English *mine* and *thine* were regularly used instead of *my* and *thy* in front of nouns beginning with vowel sounds. This use survived in poetry long after it became unfashionable in prose. For example, the phrase 'thine enemies' is found some 40 times in the 1611 version of the Bible. In about the same period the poet Ben Jonson wrote, 'Drink to me only with thine eyes'. Two and a half centuries later, the Battle Hymn of the American Republic began, 'Mine eyes have seen the glory of the coming of the Lord'.

One is a third person singular pronoun used for an indefinite subject, as in 'One cannot expect fine weather in August.' The French use *On* in the same way. It has an accusative and dative form *one* and a possessive form *one's*. The subject *one* must not be referred to later in a sentence as *him, his* or *her; one* or *one's* must be used – eg, 'One cannot expect fine weather for *one's* holidays in August.'

Personal pronouns with '-self', as in myself, yourself, have two distinct meanings:

1. as *emphasizing* words attached to a noun or to another pronoun – eg, '*I* saw him *myself*' or '*I myself* saw him'.
2. as *reflexive* pronouns acting as objects or indirect objects – eg, 'He hurt *himself*'; 'You must blame *yourselves* for this'; '(You) Help *yourselves*'. Reflexive pronouns are used when a subject does something to himself; they have the boomerang effect of bouncing back an action on to the subject who performs it.

Other languages use different words for these two meanings.

Relative Pronouns

The words most commonly used as relative pronouns are: *who* (*whom* in the accusative and *whose* in the genitive), used about people; *which*, used about things; and *that*, used about people and things.

The use of these relative pronouns introduces a new technical term – *clauses*. When sentences are joined together to become parts of one larger sentence, they are called its clauses. The simplest way of joining two clauses is with a conjunction like *and*, as in the two examples below:

1. There was an old woman *and* she lived in a shoe.
2. She lived in a shoe *and* she made it a home for her family.

Another way of joining two clauses is with a relative pronoun. Clauses beginning with relative pronouns are called *relative clauses*.

A relative pronoun performs two functions: it acts as a conjunction, joining its clause to another clause; and it also acts as a pronoun, avoiding repetition of a noun already used in the previous clause. This can be illustrated by using relative pronouns instead of the conjunction *and* in the two examples:

1. There was an old woman, *who* lived in a shoe.
2. She lived in a shoe, *which* she made a home for her family.

At this point we need to use another new technical term – *antecedent*. The word means literally 'going before'. In this context it refers to the previously used ('going before') noun which a relative pronoun stands for. This noun is called the *antecedent of the relative pronoun*.

In the first sentence *who* is a conjunction joining the two clauses, and it is also a pronoun standing for *old woman* (its antecedent). Similarly in the second sentence, *which* is a conjunction joining the two clauses, and it is also a pronoun standing for *shoe* (its antecedent).

The question of the *case of a relative pronoun* (in what case is *who* or *which*, and why is it in that case?) is particularly important when you are studying a foreign language. It can often be important in English too – when deciding whether to say *who* or *whom*. The principle to remember is:

> *The case of a relative pronoun is decided by its function in its own clause, and not by the case of its antecedent.*

Look again at the first of the two examples we have been considering: 'There was an old woman, who lived in a shoe.' The relative clause is – *who* (ie, *she* = the old woman) *lived in a shoe*. Clearly in this clause *who* is the subject of *lived* and so in the nominative case.

The case of the antecedent *old woman* in the first clause of this sentence is, as it happens, also nominative; but if we change the sentence to 'I met an old woman who lived in a shoe', you will see that in the first clause the antecedent *old woman* is now in the accusative case (object of *met*), while the relative clause with its subject *who* and verb *lived* is quite unchanged.

The same principle can be applied to the second of our two examples: 'She lived in a shoe, which she made a home for her family.' The relative clause is – *which* (ie, *it* = the shoe) *she made a home for her family*. With a slight rearrangement, you will see that this means *she made which* (ie, *it* = the shoe) *a home for her family*. It is now clear that in this clause *which* is the object of *made* and so in the accusative case.

What I have said about finding the case of relative pronouns may be briefly summarized like this:

1. Isolate the relative clause.
2. Replace the relative pronoun by the appropriate personal pronoun: he, him, his; she, her; it, its; they, them, their.
3. Rearrange the clause if the sense requires it. The case should then be clear.

English is very flexible in its use of relative clauses. Notice the various ways in which the relative clause is expressed in a third example:

The shoe
$\begin{cases} \textit{in which the old woman lived} \\ \textit{which the old woman lived in} \\ \textit{that the old woman lived in} \\ \textit{the old woman lived in} \end{cases}$
was too small for her family.

In the last form of the relative clause, the relative pronoun has been omitted altogether. This is not uncommon in English, but never happens in other languages.

Finally, here are two words which sometimes function as relative pronouns without being recognized as such:

what – when it means 'the thing which' or 'the things which' – combines antecedent and relative in one word. For example:

'What (the thing which) I tell you three times is true' (Lewis Carroll).

As may be a relative pronoun when it has an antecedent including 'such' or 'same' or another 'as'. For example:

This has not been *such* a good Christmas	*as* I had last year.
You sent me the *same* card	*as* I sent you.
I have not had *as* many gifts	*as* my sister (had).

You will find more about relative clauses in Chapter 17: see the section *Relative Clauses of Two Types*.

Interrogative Pronouns

As their name implies, interrogative pronouns are used to ask questions – *Who? Whom? Whose? What? Which?* You will recognize them all as words which made their appearance in the last section as relative pronouns. The following examples show interrogative pronouns in action:

1. *Who* goes there? (Subject: nominative)
2. *Whose* book is that? (Possessive: genitive)
3. *What* happened yesterday? (Subject: nominative)
4. *Which* of these books did you enjoy most? (Direct Object: accusative)

In examples three and four *what* and *which* are used by themselves as interrogative pronouns. When either of these words is used immediately before a noun, it becomes an interrogative adjective. (*What event* happened? *Which book* did you enjoy?) Further illustrations of interrogative adjectives will be found in Chapter 6.

Whom should, strictly speaking, be used instead of *Who* whenever the sentence requires it to be an object:

1. *Whom* did you meet yesterday? (Direct object of the verb *meet*; accusative)
2. *To whom* did you give the book? (Object of the preposition *to*; accusative); or, the same question with a different word-order:
3. *Whom* did you give the book to? (Object of the preposition *to*; accusative)

In sentences one and three *who* is accepted instead of *whom* in modern colloquial English. In sentence two, and in similar sentences, *whom* should always be used (*of whom, about whom, from whom,* etc).

Demonstrative Pronouns

An old jingle speaks of demonstrative words as '*This* and *that* and their plurals *these* and *those*'. As their name suggests, the function of these words is to *point out* things or people and draw our attention to them. The same words may be used as pronouns and also as adjectives (see Chapter 6 for demonstrative adjectives). In this chapter we are concerned with demonstrative pronouns.

Demonstrative pronouns are substitutes for nouns – and at the same time point out the people or things concerned. Sometimes they refer to people or things already mentioned. For example:

I like our garden better than *that* of our neighbours. (*that* = the garden)

Sometimes they refer to people or things that are about to be mentioned. For example:

That is my cousin's house, and *these* are his children. (*that* = the house; *these* = the children)

A demonstrative pronoun may also refer to a group of words expressing a single thought and so regarded as equivalent to a noun. For example:

You must buy your ticket in advance; *this* is essential. (*this* is a shorthand way of saying: buying-your-ticket-in-advance.)

Other Pronouns

Here is a selection of other pronouns. Most of them are also adjectives, and the two uses of these words are illustrated below.

Any: I have not read *any* of your books. (pronoun)
Any time's kissing time. (adjective)

Each: I have many friends; *each* is dear to me. (pronoun)
Each elector has one vote. (adjective)

Either: Here are two dictionaries; *either* is suitable for your studies. (pronoun)
You will find *either* book useful. (adjective)

Neither: *Neither* of these two films is intended for children. (pronoun)
Neither story is convincing. (adjective)

None: This little piggy had roast beef; this little piggy had *none*. (pronoun)
(*None* as an adjective is archaic; *none other gods* occurs in the Prayer Book of 1662.)

Other(s): These men merely talk: *others* act. (pronoun)
'This *other* Eden, demi-paradise.' (adjective)

Some: I have no ink; you have *some*. (pronoun)
Some newspapers are tabloids. (adjective)

You should bear in mind the following points:

1. *Each* refers to several people or things, as the examples show.
2. *Either* and *neither* are used when only two are involved.
3. When *each, either* and *neither* are used as subject pronouns or as adjectives with subject nouns, they must be followed by singular verbs, as in the examples.
4. *None* is treated by modern dictionaries as singular or plural as the sense requires. For example:

    Have you any ink? There *is none* in my pen. (*not any*)
    None but members of the society *are* allowed to vote. (*no persons*)
5. In addition to their use as pronouns and adjectives, some of these words have further functions. For example, *either* and *neither* are also conjunctions.

Summary of Pronouns

This chapter has dealt with the five groups of pronouns:

1. Personal pronouns
2. Relative pronouns
3. Interrogative pronouns
4. Demonstrative pronouns
5. Other pronouns.

6

Adjectives

Definition
Adjectives describe nouns and pronouns.

This is sometimes expressed by saying that adjectives *qualify*, meaning that they add qualities to, nouns and pronouns; or that adjectives *limit* nouns and pronouns (in 'white horses' the adjective 'white' limits the noun 'horses' to those of a particular colour). These three definitions, describe, qualify and limit, are all helpful in understanding the function of adjectives.

The most easily recognized adjectives add such qualities as:

Size – a *tall* building: a *vast* cathedral: a *wide-ranging* enquiry: a *tiny* tot.

Colour – the *Red* Cross: a *swarthy* complexion: *pale* ale: *white* horses.

Number and Amount – *all* creatures: *enough* money: *thirty* days: the *third* man. (All the numerals – ie, numbers – are adjectives when they are used to qualify nouns. Cardinal numbers is the grammatical name for those which answer the question *How many?* – eg, seven, thirty, a thousand. Ordinal numbers show the *order* – eg, seventh, thirtieth, thousandth.)

There are countless other adjectives that add similar descriptive detail to their nouns or pronouns: for example, a *busy* street, a *strong* arm, a *beautiful* scene, a *good* cause, a *bad* example.

The Position of Adjectives
An adjective may be used in two positions in a sentence:

1. directly attached to its noun and usually preceding

25

the noun, as in 'the *leaning* tower of Pisa'; sometimes closely following the noun, as in the line of poetry 'The river Weser, *deep* and *wide*' ('The Pied Piper of Hamelin'). Such adjectives must be directly attached *to their own nouns*. Consider the unflattering wording of an advertisement for '*Outsize* Ladies' Dresses' instead of 'Ladies' *Outsize* Dresses'.

2. joined to its noun by a verb – eg, 'The tower of Pisa *is impressive*'; The river *is* (or *seems*, *looks*) *deep*. In this position an adjective is called *predicative*, because it helps the verb to form the predicate of a sentence.

The adjectives so far mentioned in this chapter are words that are obviously descriptive; they add size, colour, number and other qualities to nouns. The rest of the chapter will deal with adjectives which may be less easy to identify or which require special explanation. They are arranged in the following sections:

Comparison of Adjectives
Interrogative Adjectives
Demonstrative Adjectives
Articles
Some Other Adjectives

Comparison of Adjectives

This is also known as *the three degrees of comparison of adjectives*, a technical term for the three stages, or degrees of power, which many adjectives possess.

The *positive* degree is the ordinary form of an adjective – eg, *busy*.

The *comparative* degree is used to compare two individuals or groups – eg, *busier* or *more busy*. 'A city is *busier* (*more busy*) than a village.'

The *superlative* degree is used to mark the most outstanding of *more than two* eg, *busiest* and *most busy*. 'Of all my friends he is the *busiest* (*most busy*).'

Some adjectives prefer to form their comparatives and superlatives with *-er* and *-est* endings. Others, especially long adjectives, always use *more* and *most*. For example:

Positive	Comparative	Superlative
strong	stronger	strongest
beautiful	more beautiful	most beautiful

A few well-known adjectives have unexpected forms for their comparatives and superlatives. For example:

Positive	Comparative	Superlative
good	better	best
bad	worse	worst
little	less	least
much, many	more	most

(*Little* and *much* with their comparatives and superlatives are also used as adverbs. See the *Comparison of Adverbs*, Chapter 13.)

The comparative adjective *less* means either *smaller*, as in 'This is of *less* importance', or *a smaller amount of*, as in 'Take *less* jam on your bread'. A common mistake is to use *less* with a plural word to mean *fewer*. For example, we should say 'There were *fewer* (not *less*) spectators at the match.'

A kind of reverse form of the comparative and superlative is produced by using the adverbs *less* and *least* in front of an adjective. For example:

Positive	Comparative	Superlative
busy	less busy	least busy

Interrogative Adjectives

The interrogative adjectives, *what* and *which*, ask for information about their nouns, such as '*What* timetable do you follow during the day?' and '*Which* subject do you enjoy most?' They may often be regarded as 'blank-cheque' adjectives asking to be filled out with a noun's qualities, as in the following illustration:

Question: *Which* book have you chosen?

Answer: The *large, red, well-printed* one.

(For the use of *what* and *which* as interrogative pronouns see Chapter 5.)

What is also used in *exclamations*. The difference between a question and an exclamation is shown by the tone of voice in speaking, and by the punctuation and the word order in writing. For example:

Question: *What* nonsense have you written today?
Exclamation: *What* nonsense you have written today!

Demonstrative Adjectives

Demonstrative adjectives are used for *pointing out* the nouns to which they are attached. They are *this, that, these* and *those*. '*This* book is my favourite' and '*Those* gardens are beautiful in spring.' (These words may also be employed as demonstrative pronouns – see Chapter 5.)

Articles

Articles – *the, a* and *an* – are adjectives. *The* is called the *definite article*: it gives an individual quality to a noun. *The* book means a particular book.

A and *an* are forms of the *indefinite article* and are used with the opposite effect. *A* is used before words beginning with a consonant (a book, a horse), and before words beginning with a consonant-sound (a university, a one-armed bandit). *An*, of course, is used before words beginning with a vowel sound (an adjective, an heiress). A very few words beginning with *h* have two pronunciations according to whether or not the *h* is sounded; for instance, it's a matter of personal preference whether you say 'a *h*otel' or 'an 'otel'.

Some Other Adjectives

Here are a few other common adjectives, which are sometimes overlooked because of their familiarity. Each is followed by a noun:

any time, *each* day, *every* direction, *either* book, *neither* team, *other* suggestions, *some* petrol, *no* man's land.

Most of these words, like interrogative and demonstrative adjectives, can be pronouns (when they are substitutes for nouns). Examples of these two uses are given side by side in the section *Other Pronouns* in the previous chapter.

The word *no* may also be used as the opposite of *yes*. It is then considered to be an adverb. (See Chapter 13, *Everyday Adverbs*.)

Summary of Adjectives

1. Adjectives may be defined as describing, qualifying or limiting nouns and pronouns.
2. Easily recognizable adjectives include those of size, colour, number and amount.
3. The two positions of adjectives.
4. The comparison of adjectives: the positive, comparative and superlative degrees.
5. Interrogative adjectives ask for information about their nouns.
6. Demonstrative adjectives point out their nouns.
7. Definite and indefinite articles.
8. Some other adjectives.

7

Introducing Verbs: Sentences II

The Romans, being themselves practical men of action, regarded the verb as the most important part of their speech, since most verbs are *action*-words, which may be called verbs of *doing*. This explains why they named it *the* word (*verbum* in Latin, which became the French *verbe*, the Italian and Spanish *verbo* and the English *verb*).

However, though the vast majority of verbs can be described as action-words, there are also two minority groups of verbs which do not come under this heading. These are verbs of *being* (link-verbs), and *auxiliary* (helping) verbs. This chapter will look at each of these three groups in turn.

A concluding section of the chapter (*Sentences II*) examines predicates of four types, and shows how they may be arranged in tabular form.

Verbs of Doing

These verbs are either *transitive* (used with a direct object) or *intransitive* (used without a direct object).

Transitive refers to the action of a verb 'going across' to its object which follows (*trans* in Latin means *across*; and *-itive* means *going*). You may like to picture the action as jumping the gap between verb and object like an electric spark. For example:

Subject	Verb	Direct Object
The musician	played	the piano
We	enjoy	ice cream

Intransitive of course refers to the action of a verb which does not 'move across' to affect a direct object. For example:

Subject	Verb
Heavy rain	fell
A bomb	exploded

You will realize that some verbs can be used in either a transitive or an intransitive way. *Play*, for instance, used transitively in the first of the four examples above, becomes intransitive in 'The children *played* in the garden', since the verb has no direct object in this sentence. Conversely, the verb *explode*, used intransitively in the last example above, becomes transitive in 'The bomb squad *exploded* the bomb'.

Since action-verbs form the great majority of all verbs, the later verb chapters (8 to 12) will deal mainly with verbs of this type.

Verbs of Being (Link-Verbs)

These are non-technical descriptions of what grammarians call *intransitive verbs of incomplete predication*. They are incomplete because they need to be followed by a completing word, called a *complement*; and their function is to link a subject with a complement.

Here are some sentences using verbs of this kind. If you leave out the complements, you will realize at once why these verbs by themselves are called incomplete.

Subject	Link-Verb	Complement
The sky	was	blue (adjective)
This	is	he (pronoun)
Tomorrow	will be	Monday (noun)
His enemies	seemed	victorious (adjective)
The mob	became	excited (adjective)

The commonest link-verbs are the ones used in these sentences. They are: *to be* (was, is, will be); *to seem*; and *to become*. They are sometimes called verbs of being, because verbs of this kind have the same basic meaning as the verb *to be*. You can test this by substituting *were* and *was* for the verbs in the last two sentences of the examples. Several other verbs can be used as link-verbs (though this is not their ordinary meaning): the sea *grew* rough; the traveller *turned* pale; she *looked* happy; the experiment *proved* successful. These all pass the same test – the verb *was* may be substituted for each of these verbs.

The complements are called *predicative* nouns, adjectives or pronouns. Because they are identified with their subjects, they are said to *agree with their subjects in case*. Therefore in these sentences the complements are in the nominative case. This explains why it is grammatically correct to say 'It is I' and 'This is he' (though *me* and *him* are commonly used in colloquial English).

A few *passive verbs* (*passive* is explained in Chapter 9) are used exactly like these link-verbs. For example:

She *was elected* a member of Parliament.

He *was appointed* chairman.

He *is named* John.

Instead of a noun, adjective or pronoun complement, an adverb or adverb-phrase (a group of words doing the job of an adverb) can perform the completing function for a verb of being. For example:

His enemies were *there*. (adverb)

His enemies were *in the town*. (adverb phrase)

(Note: the verb *to be* has two other uses besides being a link-verb. These are covered in the next section.)

Auxiliary (Helping) Verbs

This name is given to a few verbs when they are merely *helping to form the tenses of other verbs*. (Tenses are discussed in Chapter 10. At present it is only necessary to know that verbs change their forms to show the time when they happen; these forms are called tenses.)

It is important to understand that each of these auxiliary verbs can also be a full verb with a meaning of its own. Here is a selection of auxiliary verbs with examples. Below each of them you will see how the same words can also be full verbs with their own meanings.

1. *Have, had, shall have*

As auxiliary verbs, these help to form past tenses – eg, I *have* (he *has*) finished; They *had* arrived; We *shall have* (you *will have*) written. (Notice here and in other examples below that some tenses require two auxiliary verbs – eg, '*shall have* written'.)

As a verb with its own full meaning, *have* basically means *possess* (see a dictionary for other meanings). Notice that *have* in this sense is a *present* tense (I have something *now*). The other tenses are:

Past: I have had, I was having, I had, I did have, I had had.
Futures: I shall have, I shall have had.

2. *Shall, will*
As auxiliary verbs, both of these help to form future tenses – eg, I *shall* (you *will*) finish; We *shall have* (you *will have*) written.

As a verb with its own full meaning, *will* contains the idea of using one's willpower to achieve something eg, She *willed* her money to charity; He *willed* himself to remain calm; I *will* (answer in the marriage service).

3. *Should, would*
These are the past tenses of the auxiliaries *shall* and *will*. For example, the sentence 'He says that he *will* write' becomes in past time 'He said that he *would* write'. *Should* and *would* also help to form subjunctive and conditional tenses (see Chapter 11).

As a verb with its own full meaning, *should* means *ought to*, as in 'You *should* take your umbrella. It's going to rain'. *Would* means *was determined* (to), as in 'She *would* go. No one could stop her'. *Would* also refers to a past habit or custom, as in 'All his life he *would* get up at six o'clock in the morning'.

4. *May, might*
As auxiliaries *may* and its past tense *might* help to form Subjunctive tenses (see Chapter 11). Among other meanings the subjunctive expresses wishes, as in 'May the best man win'.

With its own full meaning, *may* contains the ideas of possibility and permission – eg, They *may* arrive tomorrow; *May* I have some more cake?; Yes, you *may*.

5. *Be*

As an auxiliary verb *be* helps to form tenses of all verbs – eg, They *were* writing; It *has been* finished.

In its own right, *be* is a link verb – eg, The sky *was* blue. It also means *exist*, as in 'To *be* or not to *be*' and 'There *is* a green hill far away'.

All the tenses of *be* may be used in both ways. They are:
Present: I am, you are, etc.
Past: I have been, I was, I had been.
Future: I shall be, I shall have been.

6. *Do, does, did*

As auxiliary verbs, these help to form the tenses of all verbs except the verb *be* – eg, She *does* work hard; *Did* they arrive?

In its own right, *do* in all its tenses means to *perform an action* – eg, The girl *was doing* her homework. You will find many further meanings in a dictionary.

7. *Let*

As an auxiliary, *let* helps to form the imperative (see Chapter 11) – eg, *Let's* forget it.

With its full meaning, *let* means *allow* or *permit* (to) – eg, His mother *will* not *let* him watch television. It also means the action of a landlord – eg, House to *let*.

Sentences II: Objects and Complements

In the final section (*Sentences I*) of Chapter 4 we saw that each sentence contains two main parts: the *subject*, naming the person(s) or thing(s) the sentence is speaking about; and the *predicate*, which says something about the subject, and whose essential component is the verb. We are now able to distinguish predicates of four different kinds:

1. containing a transitive verb and its direct object – eg, We *enjoy ice cream*.
2. containing a transitive verb and its indirect object as well as its direct object – eg, She *told her sister this story*. (The indirect object is *her sister*, which is equivalent to *to her sister*. See the *Dative Case* in Chapter 4.)

3. containing an intransitive verb and making complete sense without any additional words – eg, Birds *sing*.
4. containing a link-verb (verb of being) and its complement – eg, The sky *was blue*. The complement may be a noun or adjective or pronoun. It *completes* the sense of a verb like *was*; here the adjective *blue* is the complement. Because of their important roles in their predicates, complements are often called *predicative* nouns, adjectives or pronouns.

The various parts of the sentences in this section may be tabulated like this:

Subject and Predicate Table

SUBJECT	PREDICATE			
	Verb	Direct Object	Indirect Object	Complement
We	enjoy	ice cream		
She	told	this story	(to) her sister	
Birds	sing			
The sky	was			blue

One further addition may be made to simple sentences like these. That is the adverb or adverbial phrase which sometimes qualifies the predicate. An explanation of this will be found in the section called *Sentences III* of Chapter 13.

Summary of Verbs
1. Verbs of doing are either transitive (used with a direct object) or intransitive (used without a direct object).
2. Verbs of being are link-verbs. Their function is to link a subject with a complement.
3. Auxiliary (helping) verbs help to form the tenses of other verbs. But some verbs used in this way also possess full independent meanings of their own.
4. Verbs of doing and being may be used in sentences with predicates of four kinds. In *Sentences II*, four examples are arranged in tabular form to make their structure plain.

8

Naming the Parts of a Verb

Verb Table 1 shows the various parts of a verb without explanations or examples; these will be given in the following chapters.

Verb Table 1
The Parts of a Verb

	FINITE	
INDICATIVE mood	*ACTIVE VOICE* SUBJUNCTIVE & CONDITIONAL moods	IMPERATIVE mood
INDICATIVE mood	*PASSIVE VOICE* SUBJUNCTIVE & CONDITIONAL moods	IMPERATIVE mood
	NON-FINITE	
INFINITIVES	*ACTIVE VOICE* PARTICIPLES	GERUNDS
INFINITIVES	*PASSIVE VOICE* PARTICIPLES	GERUNDS

Note: Each of these parts will be explained as follows:
Finite and Non-Finite   Chapter 8
Active and Passive Voices   Chapter 9
Indicative Mood   Chapter 10
Subjunctive, Conditional and Imperative Moods   Chapter 11
Infinitives, Participles, Gerunds   Chapter 12

Finite and Non-Finite

First, it is necessary to understand the main division of a verb into a *finite* part and a *non-finite part*. Finite means 'limited' or 'restricted'. (A person sometimes says rather pompously, 'My resources are finite' when he means 'I have only a limited amount of money to spend.') In the finite part of a verb, the verb's action is *restricted to a particular subject*.

For example, 'hear' is a verb; but in the sentence 'The dog *hears* his master's voice', *hears* is called a finite verb because it belongs to and is limited to its subject noun, *the dog*. This is summed up in the following:

Definition: A finite verb has a subject, and it agrees with its subject in person and number.

Person and number were explained in the section about personal pronouns in Chapter 5. Here they are found in the simplest tense of a finite verb, which is called the present indicative tense:

First person singular	I hear
Second person singular	you hear (*old form:* thou hearest)
Third person singular	he, she *or* it hears (*old form:* heareth)
First person plural	we hear
Second person plural	you hear (*old form:* ye hear)
Third person plural	they hear

In our sentence 'The dog hears his master's voice', the verb is third person singular in agreement with (because it belongs to) its subject, *the dog* (represented in the tense by the singular pronoun *he*, *she* or *it*). If we change the subject to *the dogs* (ie, *they*), the verb becomes *hear* (third person plural). As these examples show, noun subjects are either third person singular or third person plural.

Most English verbs do not show their agreement by a change of ending except in the old second person singular (thou hear*est*) and in the third person singular (he, she or it hear*s*). However, in other languages you may find up to six different verb endings in a tense like this.

The Finite Parts of a Verb

These are the *indicative* mood, which makes statements of fact; the *subjunctive* mood, which expresses ideas, such as wishes, suppositions and purposes; the *conditional* tenses, which are regarded either as forming a separate (conditional) mood or as part of the subjunctive mood; and the *imperative* mood, which gives orders.

Mood is derived from the same Latin word as *mode*, meaning *way* or *manner*. As a grammatical term, the word *moods* names a verb's 'attitudes' or ways of speaking. For practical purposes it is sufficient to speak simply of 'the indicative' instead of 'the indicative mood'.

The Non-Finite Parts of a Verb

These are the parts of a verb which cannot agree with a subject in person and number. They are *infinitives* – eg, '*to* hear'; *participles*, which are *verbal adjectives* – eg, 'a *smoking* fire'; and *gerunds*, which are *verbal nouns* – eg, '*Smoking* is bad for you.'

Summary of the Parts of a Verb

Verb Table 1 shows the various parts of a verb.

1. In its finite parts a verb has a subject, with which it agrees in person and number.
2. In its non-finite parts a verb cannot agree with a subject in person and number.

9

Active Verbs and Passive Verbs

The technical names of these two parts of a verb are the *active voice* and the *passive voice*, but it is sufficient to say the *active and the passive*.

The Active Voice
These four sentences illustrated *verbs of doing* in Chapter 7:

1. The musician *played* the piano.
2. We *enjoy* ice cream.
3. Heavy rain *fell*.
4. A bomb *exploded*.

As we have seen, sentences one and two are transitive verbs because they have direct objects, while three and four are intransitive verbs because they have their full meaning without a direct object.

All four verbs, however, are called *active verbs*, because in each sentence the subject (musician, we, rain, bomb) *performs an action*.

The Passive Voice
Sentences one and two can be put in a different way:

1. The piano *was played* by the musician.
2. Ice cream *is enjoyed* by us.

In this case the two verbs are called *passive*, a word meaning 'suffering' or 'enduring', because the subject is described as *suffering rather than performing the action*.

You can see what has happened: the direct objects of the active verbs (*piano, ice cream*) have now become the subjects of passive verbs. A sentence containing an active transitive verb and its object can always be made passive in this way without altering its meaning.

But this process of reversal cannot be applied to sentences three and four. The reason is that the active verbs in three and four are intransitive, ie, they are complete in themselves and do not have direct objects, and so there are no new subjects available if we try to make them passive.

Hence the rule: *transitive verbs can be used in the passive but intransitive verbs do not have a passive.*

Many verbs, like *explode*, can be used both intransitively and transitively. The two different meanings are marked in the dictionaries as v.i. (verb intransitive) and v.t. (verb transitive), and must be carefully distinguished. In sentence four above, 'The bomb exploded', the verb *exploded* is intransitive because the sentence does not say that the bomb caused an object to explode; the action is complete without an object. However, the same verb is used transitively when we say 'The bomb squad exploded the bomb' because the action now has a direct object. This transitive use of the verb can be expressed in the passive without altering the meaning of the sentence: 'The bomb was exploded by the bomb squad'. As in sentences one and two above, the direct object of the active verb has now become the subject of the passive verb.

Prepositional Verbs

Sometimes an intransitive verb is used so closely with a preposition that the verb-and-preposition unit is treated as a transitive verb: it takes a direct object and can be used in the passive. Here are a few examples:

Laugh at
They all *laughed at* him. (Active)
He was *laughed at* by them all. (Passive)

Listen to
We *listened to* him attentively. (Active)
He *was listened to* attentively by us. (Passive)

Speak to
Nobody *speaks to* them. (Active)
They *are* not *spoken to* by anybody. (Passive)

Passive Verbs in English with a Direct Object

Only in English is it possible for a passive verb to have a direct object. This is a peculiarly English sentence structure which can never be used in other languages.

Here is a sentence with an active verb and two objects of different kinds:

His mother	told	(to) him	a bedtime story
(subject)	(active verb)	(indirect object)	(direct object)

When we make this sentence passive in the way that we did sentences one and two at the beginning of this chapter, it becomes:

A bedtime story	was told	(to) him	by his mother
(subject)	(passive verb)	(indirect object)	

In English, however, it is possible, and more idiomatic, to use another method to make the sentence passive:

He	was told	a bedtime story	by his mother
(subject)	(passive verb)	(direct object)	

In other words, the *indirect* object has turned into the subject of the passive verb; and the old direct object has been retained as the object of the passive verb. It must be stressed that this can only be done in English. An English student of a foreign language is tempted to translate this type of sentence literally into a language such as Latin, French or German.

Note: The sentences used as illustrations in this chapter all contain finite verbs. The active and the passive are also found in the non-finite parts of verbs. See Verb Table 5 in Chapter 12.

Summary of Active and Passive Voices in the Finite Parts of a Verb

1. The subject of an active verb performs an action.
2. The subject of a passive verb *suffers* an action performed by someone or something else.

3. A sentence containing an active verb which is *transitive* (used with a direct object) can be rewritten using a passive verb with the previous direct object as its subject. An intransitive verb does not have a passive.
4. There are a few cases of *intransitive-verbs-and-prepositions* being treated as equivalent to transitive verbs (prepositional verbs).
5. The use of a passive verb with a direct object is a peculiarity of English.

10

The Tenses of the Indicative

Verb Table 2
The Tenses of the Indicative

The Verb Table shows the tenses of the indicative and should be used side by side with the explanations in Chapter 10.

Where a tense has an alternative form emphasizing *continuous* action, this form has been printed in brackets.

At the foot of the page, the present indicative active tense, which has already appeared in Chapter 8, is repeated, with archaic forms in brackets. Using this as a model, you will be able to complete all the tenses in the Verb Table.

TENSE	ACTIVE	PASSIVE
Present	I hear *or* I do hear (I am hearing)	I am heard (I am being heard)
Perfect	I have heard (I have been hearing)	I have been heard
Imperfect	I was hearing	I was heard (I was being heard)
Past Definite	I heard *or* I did hear	I was heard
Pluperfect	I had heard (I had been hearing)	I had been heard
Future	I shall hear, you *will* hear	I shall be heard, you *will* be heard
Future Perfect	I shall have heard, etc. (I shall have been hearing)	I shall have been heard, etc.

The Present Indicative Active Tense in Full

First Person Singular	I hear
Second Person Singular	you hear (thou hearest)
Third Person Singular	he, she *or* it hears (heareth)
First Person Plural	we hear
Second Person Plural	you hear (ye hear)
Third Person Plural	they hear

The finite part of a verb consists of three *moods*, which may be described as the verb's attitudes or ways of speaking. They are: the indicative, the subjunctive (including the conditional) and the imperative. These have already been referred to in Chapter 8 and will now be more fully explained. The present chapter is about the indicative; the next chapter (11) will deal with the other moods.

The Indicative Mood
This is used to make statements of fact and, by changing the position of its subject, to ask questions about facts. For example, 'I have heard his voice' is a statement; and 'Have I heard his voice?' is a question.

You will see in Verb Table 2 that the indicative has seven active tenses and seven passive tenses. The word *tense*, derived from the Latin *tempus* which means 'time', shows the time when an action of the verb happens. Here are the tenses, with a few comments about each of them and some examples:

1. *Present Tense*: notice its three forms in the active and two in the passive. Two of these, *I am hearing* and *I am being heard*, describe *continuous* present action.

   The alternative active form, *I do hear*, is usually emphatic. (Try saying it to yourself with a stress on *do*.) It is also very common in its question form (*Do you hear?*) and with 'not' (*I do not hear*).

2. *Perfect Tense*: this is close to present time and indeed an alternative name for it is the *present perfect tense*. An Italian name is the 'very near' past (*passato prossimo*). The perfect tense is formed with the auxiliary verb *have*. In some languages (eg, French and Italian) it is a great favourite as a conversational past tense, used instead of 4 below.

3. *Imperfect Tense*: this is the *continuous past tense*; it is called 'imperfect' because it describes an unfinished action. It is a background or descriptive tense, often used to picture a scene or situation. For example: 'Outside the house the sky *was becoming* gloomy, the rain *was falling* heavily and the wind *was howling; inside, a fire was blazing* on the hearth. Grandpa *was sleeping* in his favourite chair, and everything *was* warm and comforting . . .'

4. *Past Definite Tense*: this is used to describe past events. For example: '. . .Suddenly someone *knocked* loudly

on the door. The sound *thundered* through the quiet house and Grandpa *started* out of his sleep. . .'

Here we have a series of actions or happenings, which took place against the background described by the previous (imperfect) tense – somewhat like actors making their entrances on a stage set.

The alternative form of this tense, *I did hear*, is emphatic; it is also used in the question form (*Did you hear?*) and with 'not' (*I did not hear*). In other words, it works like its present tense equivalent, *I do hear*.

The past definite tense has a number of different names, even in English. It is also called *past historic, preterite* and *past absolute*.

5. *Pluperfect Tense*: this uses the auxiliary verb *had*, which places its action further back in time than the other past actions in a sentence. For example: 'We *had* just *entered* the room when we were startled by a shout. "Who's that?" cried Grandpa.' The pluperfect (*had entered*) happened before the two past definite actions (*were startled* and *cried*).

6. *Future Tense*: this of course puts the action in the future, as in 'I shall hear'. It is sometimes known as the *future simple tense* to distinguish it from 7 below.

7. *Future Perfect Tense*: this tense is used to describe an action which will have been performed by a certain time, as in 'I shall have heard by Monday'.

The difference in time between the future perfect and the future simple is usually self-evident – eg, 'I *shall have finished* my work by 10 o'clock; after that I *shall come* to see you.'

In the English usage it is idiomatic to leave out the *shall* when the future perfect is used in certain clauses – eg, 'When I (*shall*) *have* finished my work, I shall come and see you.' The same holds true for similar clauses beginning '*If* I (shall) have finished. . .'; '*After* I (shall) have finished. . .'; '*As soon as* I (shall) have finished. . .' and so on. But there is not an equivalent usage to this in many other languages, such as French, Italian and Latin.

Continuous Forms

The continuous forms of some active tenses, which are printed in brackets in Verb Table 2, must not be confused with passive tenses. 'I am hearing' (present active tense), for example, is quite different from 'I am heard' (present passive tense).

Archaic Forms

Old forms that are no longer in general use are called archaic. In all tenses of the verb the original second-person-singular forms with *thou* as the subject were common currency in Elizabethan English; and they survived in poetry into the present century. In ordinary speech the *you*-form of the plural has replaced the *thou*-form, so that the second persons singular and plural are now the same. In European languages generally, a similar process has been taking place, but more slowly; the old second-person-singular forms are still used among families and between close friends.

Shall or Will?

In ordinary future tenses, *shall* is used for the first persons singular and plural (*I shall* and *we shall*); and *will* is used with the second and third persons (*you, he, she, it* and *they*).

But this rule can be reversed to produce a different meaning. *I will* and *we will* mean *intend to* or *promise to*. (In a wedding service the bride and bridegroom both say *I will*.)

Using *shall* with *you, he, she, it* and *they* gives it a force which is practically the same as *must* – eg, 'Thou *shalt* not steal'; 'This book *shall* be returned to the library when it is due.'

There is a cautionary tale of a foreigner who got into difficulties while bathing at an English seaside resort. Not understanding the English use of *shall* and *will*, he shouted: 'I will drown; no one shall save me.' And no one did.

The distinction between *shall* and *will* is often neglected in colloquial English, *I/we will* being used as ordinary future expressions.

Should and Would

Here are two tenses that do not strictly belong to the Indicative mood. They have, however, a distinct resemblance to the future simple and future perfect indicative tenses, and for this reason they are introduced here.

I should hear	I should have heard
You would hear	You would have heard
He/she/it would hear	He/she/it would have heard
We should hear	We should have heard
You would hear	You would have heard
They would hear	They would have heard

(Passive: I should be heard, etc. I should have been heard, etc.)

You will notice that *should* and *would* are distinguished in the same way as *shall* and *will* in ordinary future tenses, ie, *should* with *I* and *we*, *would* with the other persons. (However, *I would* and *we would* are widely accepted today.)

The two main uses of these tenses are as follows:

1. As past forms of ordinary future tenses in sentences *reporting* what someone said or thought. Imagine that someone has said 'I *shall arrive* on Monday'. This information could be reported in such sentences as:

    He said that he *would* arrive on Monday.

    We thought that he *would* arrive on Monday.

    I believed that I *should* arrive on Monday.

    Similarly, 'I *shall have* finished my work by the weekend' will become 'I believed that I *should have* finished my work by the weekend'.

    These two new tenses are sometimes described as the future-in-the-past and the future perfect-in-the-past. These are clumsy titles, but I hope the examples make their meanings clear.

2. As the two tenses of what is called the *conditional*. This is sometimes regarded as a separate mood (the conditional mood) and sometimes as part of the subjunctive. In any case, it is found in conditional sentences that already have subjunctive tenses in

their *if* clauses. The conditional tenses will be fully explained in the next chapter.

Note: What I have said in the sections *Shall or Will?* and *Should and Would* will, I hope, be a useful simplification of a difficult subject. For further information look up these words in any good dictionary; and see also *shall, will* and *should, would* in Chambers *Pocket Guide to Good English*. There are interesting and detailed discussions of these words in Partridge's *Usage and Abusage* and Gowers' *The Complete Plain Words*.

Summary of the Tenses of the Indicative Mood

1. Verb Table 2 lists the tenses of the indicative mood, active and passive, which are explained and illustrated in this chapter.
2. Continuous forms of some tenses.
3. Archaic forms.
4. Shall/will: the different uses examined.
5. The should/would tenses.

11

The Subjunctive, the Conditional and the Imperative

The division (or *moods*) of the finite parts of the verb were shown in Verb Table 1 at the beginning of Chapter 8. The first of these, the indicative mood, has been the subject of Chapters 9 and 10. The present chapter will deal with the remaining moods.

Verb Table 3
Subjunctive and Conditional

SUBJUNCTIVE	ACTIVE	PASSIVE
Present Tense (often referring to future time)	I (may) hear I should hear I were·to hear I heard	I (may) be heard I should be heard I were to be heard
Perfect Tense	I may have heard	I may have been heard
Imperfect Tense (often referring to present time)	I might hear I should be hearing I were hearing	I might be heard I should be heard I were (being) heard
Pluperfect Tense	I had heard I might have heard I should have heard	I had been heard I might have been heard I should have been heard

CONDITIONAL (see *Should and Would* in Chapter 10)		
	ACTIVE	PASSIVE
Conditional Tense	I should hear You would hear etc.	I should be heard You would be heard etc.
Past Conditional Tense	I should have heard You would have heard etc.	I should have been heard You would have been heard etc.

The Subjunctive

Ancient grammarians invented the name *subjunctive* to describe the mood very often found in *subordinate* clauses. These clauses were regarded as being attached to the main clause of a sentence as its dependants or subordinates (*sub* meaning *under* and *-junctive* from the Latin verb meaning *join*). Unlike the indicative, which deals in facts (see Chapter 10), the subjunctive expresses *ideas*, such as wishes, some suppositions or conditions, and purposes. Most *wishes* take the form of complete short sentences: the *other subjunctives* are found in subordinate clauses dependent upon a main clause.

European languages such as French, Italian and Spanish possess exact subjunctive moods, recognizably different from their indicatives; further, there is a wide measure of agreement among native speakers of these languages about the correct use of the subjunctive. Native speakers of modern English, on the other hand, are far less subjunctive-conscious, and a major reason for this may be the existence of a wide variety of verbal forms expressing subjunctive ideas.

The Subjunctive Forms Used in English (Verb Table 3)

The *oldest surviving forms* of the English subjunctive are mostly the same as the indicative, but the words are differently used. We shall meet examples of this in conditional (*if*) clauses like:

If he *arrived* tomorrow, (I should be very surprised.)

This verb is not a past tense of the indicative but a subjunctive referring to future time and equivalent to: If he *should arrive*. . . There are also a few old forms which are different from the indicative:

1. The present active tense differs in its third person singular. The subjunctive tense is: I hear, you hear, he/she/it *hear*, etc. This form survives in *wishes* (see below) and in formal language such as:

   'The decision of the committee is that he *pay* his subscription forthwith or *cease* to be a member.'

2. The verb *to be* has its own peculiar present subjunctive, I *be*, you *be*, he/she/it *be*, etc; and its own imperfect subjunctive, I *were*, you *were*, he/she/it *were*, etc. These two tenses are particularly important as auxiliary verbs.

The other ways of forming the modern English subjunctive make use of the auxiliary verb *may* for present and future time; *might* for past time; and *should* in all tenses.

In the subjunctive, *should* is correctly used for all persons – eg, I should, you should, he/she/it should, we should, you should, they should.

The conditional tenses have already been mentioned (see *Should and Would* in Chapter 10). They prefer *would* in the second and third persons and *should* in the first persons; and they are used in the main clauses of sentences containing an *if*-plus-subjunctive subordinate clause. You will find the conditional tenses in Verb Table 3, and their use will be explained in the section below on conditions.

In the next three sections of this chapter we shall examine three ways of using subjunctive and conditional tenses:
1. The subjunctive in wishes
2. The subjunctive in subordinate conditional (*if*) clauses attached to main clauses containing one of the conditional tenses
3. The subjunctive in other subordinate clauses

The Subjunctive in Wishes
1. So *be* it! (or *May* it *be* so!)
2. God *bless* you! (or *May* God *bless* you!)
3. Hallowed *be* thy name; thy kingdom *come*; thy will *be done*. (Or *May* thy name *be* hallowed; *may* thy kingdom *come*; *may* thy will *be done*.)

In these examples are given the older forms of the subjunctive without auxiliary verbs and the same subjunctives with auxiliary verbs are given in brackets. (You can see that these subjunctive verbs are quite different from indicative statements, which would have been: 1. So *is* it. 2. God *blesses* you. 3. Hallowed *is* thy name; thy kingdom *comes*; thy will *is done*.)

All these examples use the present subjunctive (see Verb Table 3), but it is possible to use the other tenses, as follows:

4. *May* they *have arrived* in time! (Perfect)
5. If only he *were living* here now! (Imperfect)
6. If only you *had listened* to me! (Pluperfect)

The Subjunctive in Conditional (If) Clauses

What are called conditional sentences contain two parts:

1. The *if*-clause, also called the conditional clause. This is a subordinate clause naming the condition. It often comes first in the sentence, and it starts with *if* or *supposing* or, for two conditions, *whether. . .or*. For example:

> If he did that. . .
> Supposing he did that. . .
> Whether he did that or not. . .

2. The main clause of the sentence, stating what result follows from the condition. For example:

> (If he did that,) *he made a bad mistake.*

Many if-clauses, like the ones in this illustration, are completely factual and have indicative tenses. Others, which we are concerned with in this chapter, contain an element of doubt and imagination about what may happen in the *future*, as in:

if he should do that . . .

or they are fantasy about what might be happening in the *present* (but isn't), as in:

if he were doing that . . .

or about what might have happened in the *past* (but didn't), as in:

if he had done that (meaning *should have done*) . . .

If-clauses which deal with doubt, imagination or fantasy rather than with facts contain subjunctive verbs. The main clauses which accompany them generally contain one of the conditional tenses.

Here are examples of conditional (if) clauses of this kind in future, present and past time. Alongside them are the main clauses of their sentences.

Conditional Clauses

	CONDITIONAL CLAUSE/IF-CLAUSE has a subjunctive tense	MAIN CLAUSE of sentence has a conditional tense
1. Future meaning (Present Subjunctive)	If he *should do* that If he *were to do* that If he *did* that	I should help him
2. Present meaning (Imperfect Subjunctive)	If he *should be doing* that If he *were doing* that	you would be helping him
3. Past meaning (Pluperfect Subjunctive)	If he *had done* that	they would have helped him

These are typical examples of conditional clauses of the subjunctive type referring to future, present and past time. Here are a few further points to notice about them:

1. The only subjunctive forms not used in these clauses are the *may* and *might* ones.
2. The subjunctives in *If he did* and *If he had done* look like past indicative tenses, but they are in fact old surviving forms of the English subjunctive of the kind already mentioned. They represent *If he should do* (future time) and *if he should have done* (past time) respectively. This can be important in studying a foreign language.
3. The present and imperfect subjunctives in examples one and two are very similar, and there is sometimes little difference in their meanings. But the distinction between future time and present time is generally made clear by the conditional tense in the main clause: *I should help him* (tomorrow) and *You would be helping him* (today).
4. In each of the three examples the two clauses have for convenience been put in the same time: for instance, in three both are set in past time. In practice we frequently need to mix the times of the clauses. So we say:

If he had come (past), we should be enjoying his company (present). Supposing his flight were today, we should meet him at Heathrow tomorrow.

5. Two *omissions* can occur in idiomatic English. The word *If* may be omitted in such sentences as:

Were he to agree to this (= If he were to agree), we should be delighted.

Had you sent me a postcard (= If you had sent. . .), I should have met you at the station.

The whole *if-clause* is sometimes omitted and taken for granted:

I should advise you to take the job. (ie, If you asked my advice, I should advise you. . .)

6. A request or instruction (imperative mood) may replace the conditional tense of the main clause:

If you should see them tomorrow, *give* them my good wishes.

The Subjunctive in Other Subordinate Clauses

One very common type tells us the purpose or aim in somebody's mind. Here are some examples of *purpose clauses* using the present subjunctive:

1. She is telling her story in order that everyone *may know* the facts.
2. He will say nothing lest he *should be punished*.
   (in order that he *may* not *be punished*.)

The following examples show purpose clauses which use the imperfect subjunctive:

3. She told her story in order that everyone *might know* the facts.
4. He said nothing lest he *should be punished*.
   (in order that he *might not be punished*.)

The conjunctions and the conjunction phrases (see Chapter 14) which begin purpose clauses include the ones used in these sentences – *in order that* and *lest* – as well as others such as *that*, *so that*, and *in case* (which is equivalent to *lest*).

Among the subjectives in these sentences, notice that *may* (present subjunctive) in one and two changes to *might* (imperfect subjunctive) when the sentences move into the past in three and four.

Should is used in both present and past time.

Besides purpose clauses there are *many other subordinate clauses that convey ideas* (including feelings, intentions, desires). Subjunctive verbs are regularly used in these clauses, in everyday speech as well as in writing. Here are a few examples:

(She was afraid) that her husband *might desert* her.

(We are eager) that he *should be* our spokesman.

(The law requires) that the defendant *should have* a fair trial.

(The parish council requested) that an extra bus *should run* on Wednesdays.

The Imperative

Verb Table 4
Imperative

IMPERATIVE	ACTIVE	PASSIVE
One tense called the present (often refers to a future time)	Let me hear	Let me be heard
	Hear (you)	(You) Be heard
	Let him/her/it hear	Let him/her/it be heard
	Let us hear	Let us be heard
	Hear (you)	(You) Be heard
	Let them hear	Let them be heard

The imperative is the mood of the verb which gives commands.

Its name is derived from the Latin verb meaning 'command' or 'order'; *imperator*, the noun connected with the verb, was the Roman military equivalent of the modern supreme commander; this title was naturally appropriated by the rulers of the Roman Empire, and eventually became the English word 'Emperor'.

The imperative mood has one active and one passive tense (see Verb Table 4). They are often described as the *present imperative*; but their meaning obviously includes future time as well.

The most used parts are the second persons singular and plural. Both singular and plural have the same form in English – as in *Listen!* – and the subject is generally omitted, except in old English and in modern colloquial expressions. Here is an old English example from the 1611 version of the Bible: *'Choose you* this day whom you will serve.' Similar expressions in modern speech are, *'Listen you!'* and *'You listen* to me!'

The auxiliary verb *do* can help to form imperatives – *'Do tell* me'; *'Do* not (*don't*) listen to him.'

The first and third persons of the imperative (see Verb Table 4) are formed with the auxiliary verb *Let* – as in *'Let* me *see'* and *'Let* him *go.'* In other languages these *let*-forms are often expressed by the subjunctive.

Summary of the Subjunctive, Conditional and Imperative Moods

1. Together with the indicative, the moods of the finite part of the verb are: the subjunctive, the conditional and the imperative.
2. Verb Table 3 at the beginning of this chapter contains the forms of the subjunctive and conditional most frequently used in English. Most of these are illustrated in this chapter.
3. The subjunctive expresses wishes, some suppositions or conditions, and purposes.
4. The subjunctive is used in conditional clauses which contain an element of doubt, imagination or fantasy. The accompanying main clauses contain conditional tenses.
5. A common type of subordinate clause uses the subjunctive to express purpose or aim. Other subordinate clauses expressing ideas may also have subjunctive verbs.
6. The imperative is the mood which gives commands. Its forms are given in Verb Table 4.

12

The Non-Finite Parts of a Verb

Verb Table 5
Non-Finite Parts

The non-finite parts of a verb are infinitives, participles and gerunds; unlike the finite parts of a verb they do not agree in person and number with a subject (see Chapter 8). Verb Table 5 tabulates the non-finite parts. The table should be used in conjunction with Chapter 12.

INFINITIVES	ACTIVE	PASSIVE
Present Tense	to hear	to be heard
Perfect Tense	to have heard	to have been heard

PARTICIPLES	ACTIVE	PASSIVE
Present Tense	hearing	being heard
Perfect Tense	having heard	(having been) heard

GERUNDS	ACTIVE	PASSIVE
Present Tense	hearing	being heard
Perfect Tense	having heard	having been heard

Infinitives

The present infinitive active *to hear* is often called the *infinitive* of the verb 'hear'; and the equivalent of 'to hear' is the form of the verb which is listed in the dictionaries of many foreign languages.

In fact, there are four infinitives altogether, as Verb Table 5 shows. All of them are used frequently in everyday conversation. The following passage uses each of them in turn:

'I was so glad *to hear* your voice on the phone. I am pleased *to have heard* from John, too. John's ambition is *to be heard* on the radio. His father is still proud *to have been heard* singing in a pre-war promenade concert.'

In modern English the *to* of the infinitive is omitted when it follows certain other verbs. For example:

1. I need not *say* any more. (I do not need *to say*. . .)
2. We dared not *resist*. (We did not dare *to resist*.)
3. I can *tell* you the result. (I am able *to tell* you. . .)
4. You must *tell* me what you know. (You are obliged *to tell*. . .)
5. She will never let him *go*. (She will never allow him *to go*.)

(Note this use of *let* meaning allow or permit; see the section on auxiliary verbs in Chapter 7.)

Split infinitives are often mentioned but not always understood. Any part of a verb may have an adverb (or an adverbial group of words) attached to it. To 'split' an infinitive means to put this adverb between the *to* and the rest of the infinitive. For example:

1. To *frequently* forget.
2. To *completely* have been forgotten.

Though the old rule of never splitting your infinitives may be too sweeping, you are often likely to produce better English if you avoid a split infinitive. There are several ways of moving the adverb out of the danger zone:

1. *Frequently* to forget; or to forget *frequently*.
2. To have been *completely* forgotten; or to have been forgotten *completely*.

(For more information on split infinitives, see the articles in Partridge's *Usage and Abusage* and in Fowler's *Modern English Usage*.)

Participles

Participles are verbal adjectives – in other words, they are adjectives formed from verbs. There are four participles (see Verb Table 5) and they do two jobs: they help to form finite tenses; and they describe nouns and pronouns.

Forming finite tenses: If you refer to Verb Table 2 (Chapter 10) you will see that the participles *hearing, being heard* and *heard* form part of most of the indicative and many of the subjunctive tenses; the tenses are produced by combining these participles with auxiliary (helping) verbs such as I *am*, I *was*, I *have*, I *have been*. Participles also form part of some tenses of the infinitive and the gerund. In other European languages, the perfect tenses are regularly formed in a similar way.

Describing nouns and pronouns: Like all adjectives, participles describe or qualify nouns and pronouns.

Present participles are used in the following examples:

1. A *rolling* stone gathers no moss.
2. We saw a boulder *rolling* down the mountain.

These two present participles are both active. In the first sentence *rolling* describes *stone*, and in the second it describes *boulder*.

3. We watched the barrels *being rolled* into the warehouse.

Here *being rolled* is a passive present participle describing *barrels*.

Perfect participles are used in these two examples:

1. *Having spoken*, he sat down.
2. He went home, *delighted* by the enthusiasm of the audience.

In each sentence the participle describes *he*.

With objects: Because they are *verbal* adjectives, active participles of transitive verbs can have objects. In the sentence 'We watched him *playing* football', the present participle *playing* describes *him* and has the object *football*.

Participles out of control: A participle qualifies a noun or a pronoun; but, to show which noun or pronoun a participle belongs to, you must keep strict control over its position in the sentence. Otherwise, almost as if the participle had a life of its own, it can become attached to the wrong noun – or even left 'floating' without a noun at all. As a result, a sentence may acquire a meaning which was not intended or be reduced to nonsense. The following examples show what can happen:

1. '*Washing* the car, the postman brought me a letter.' This can only mean that the postman was washing the car, which is not the speaker's intention. The sentence should begin 'As I was washing. . .'
2. '*Seeing* the Cathedral tower ahead, the market-place could not be far away.' Here the participle *seeing* has completely lost its noun or pronoun. Who was doing the *seeing*? Not the *market-place*, certainly, but *some traveller who then realized that the market-place. . .*
3. 'My father was stopped by a policeman *hurrying* down the road on his way to the railway station.' Here the sense is ambiguous. It could mean that the policeman was in a hurry to catch his train. But it was probably intended to mean: '*My father, hurrying* down the road on his way to the railway station, was stopped by a policeman.'

The examples use present participles because these are the most liable to get out of control. But similar mistakes can also be made with perfect participles. The only way to avoid them is to *make sure that a participle belongs to a noun or a pronoun, and that it is placed as near to it as possible in order to make the meaning quite clear.*

Gerunds

Gerunds have exactly the same form as participles, but they are *verbal nouns*. (See Verb Table 5.) Each of the gerunds which are italicized in the examples below is acting as a noun.

1. *Smoking* is bad for your health. (Here the gerund is acting as the subject.)
2. My sister is fond of *jogging*. (As the object of the preposition *of*.)
3. We all like *being praised*. (As the object of the verb *like*.)
4. He is unhappy about *having been beaten* by his sister. (As the object of the preposition *about*.)

All these verbal nouns *name actions*; they belong to the type called abstract nouns (see Chapter 2).

Like participles, gerunds sometimes have their own objects, as in 'Smoking *cigarettes* is bad for your health'.

Summary of the Non-Finite Parts of a Verb

These are the infinitives, participles and gerunds, which are tabulated in Verb Table 5.

1. The infinitives are the forms of a verb which are preceded by *to*, but the *to* of the infinitive is omitted in modern English when it follows certain other verbs. It is usually advisable to avoid 'splitting' an infinitive, which means placing an adverb between *to* and the rest of the infinitive.

2. The participles are verbal adjectives.

   They are used together with auxiliary verbs to form most of the indicative tenses (and also many of the subjunctive and imperative forms and some tenses of the infinitive and the gerund).

   Like other adjectives, they can also qualify nouns and pronouns.

   A common mistake is to misplace a participle in a sentence (participles out of control).

3. The gerunds are verbal nouns.

13

Adverbs: Sentences III

Definition

The best starting point for a definition of adverbs is the beginning of Chapter 6. There you will find that adjectives qualify, or add qualities to, nouns and pronouns. In a similar way, *adverbs qualify any parts of speech except nouns, pronouns and interjections.* (Interjections are excluded because they have no grammatical relationship with any other words in a sentence; they cannot therefore be qualified by adverbs.) So we may say that *adverbs can qualify adjectives, other adverbs, conjunctions, prepositions and verbs.* Their most important function is to qualify *verbs*, and from this comes the term *ad*verb, meaning a word belonging *to* (*ad* in Latin) a verb.

A final section of this chapter (*Sentences III*) will illustrate the work of adverbs in qualifying the five parts of speech mentioned above.

The Various Kinds of Adverbs

Very many adverbs are formed by the addition of *-ly* to adjectives. For instance:

She has a *beautiful* voice. (adjective qualifying the noun *voice*)

She sings *beautifully*. (adverb qualifying the verb *sings*)

Adverbs of manner (see below) are often formed in this way. This chapter will deal with adverbs of the following kinds:

Adverbs of place

Adverbs of time

Adverbs of manner

Adverbs of reason and purpose

Interrogative adverbs
Conjunctive adverbs
Everyday adverbs

There will also be sections on *Adverbs According to Usage*; on *Only*; on the *Comparison of Adverbs*; and on *Adverbs in Sentences* (*Sentences III*).

Adverbs Referring to Place

These adverbs may answer questions like '*Where* do you live?' and '*Where* are you going?' Adverbs of place include: *here, there, elsewhere, nowhere*; and also the now less common words – *hence, thence, hither, thither*.

As an alternative to single-word adverbs like these, we often use *adverb phrases* like *in the house* and *to school*. These phrases consist of a preposition and a noun; they are mentioned again later in this chapter and in Chapter 15.

Adverbs Referring to Time

These adverbs may answer questions like '*When* did it happen?' Adverbs and adverb phrases of time include: *then, now, never, afterwards, always; in the morning, at 5 o'clock*.

If you have ever amused yourself telling your fortune by counting fruit stones, you probably used the following line of adverbs and adverb phrases of time: *This year, next year, sometime, never*.

Adverbs Referring to Manner

These adverbs may answer questions like '*How* did it happen?' They explain the way something happens; as we have seen above, they are often formed by adding *-ly* to adjectives.

Examples include adverbs like *slowly, stupidly, wisely, enthusiastically*; and adverb phrases such as *at high speed* (= *very quickly*), *without hesitation* (= *unhesitatingly*).

Adverbs Referring to Reason and Purpose

These adverbs may answer questions like '*Why* did it happen?' or '*What was the purpose* of doing this?' Adverbs of this kind include *purposely* and *intentionally*; and the adverb phrases like those used in the following sentences – 'They went abroad *for a holiday*' and 'He does it *to annoy*.'

Interrogative Adverbs

These adverbs are *where, when, how, why*; and the less common *whence*, meaning 'where from', and *whither*, meaning 'where to'.

These adverbs ask the questions which are answered by adverbs of place, time, manner, reason and purpose. Interrogative adverbs are 'blank-cheque' words requiring to be filled out with an adverb answer. They are like *interrogative adjectives* (Chapter 6), which often require an adjective answer.

Conjunctive Adverbs

These are the same words as interrogative adverbs (see above), but they are used in a different way. They are adverbs-which-join, and they perform two functions at the same time, as relative (or conjunctive) pronouns do. Here are three examples:

1. I cannot understand *why* you did that.
2. This is the town *where* I feel most at home.
3. You can borrow that book *when* he's read it.

See also the sentences using *when* and *where* in Chapter 14.

Everyday Adverbs

Some very common words and phrases may escape identification as adverbs because they are taken so much for granted. In this category there are a number of adverbs used to answer questions, such as *yes, certainly, of course, by all means, no* and the colloquial expression *no way*.

Other frequently used adverbs of this type include *very, too, quite, so, almost, more, scarcely, not* and *less*. These are used mainly to qualify adjectives and other adverbs. You can test this by placing each of them in front of the adjective *successful* and the adverb *successfully*.

Adverbs According to Usage

A number of words can be adverbs or some other part of speech according to the context in which they are used. *Before*, for example, can be an adverb, a preposition or a conjunction (see Chapter 15); *only* can be an adverb or an adjective. (See also *early* in the *Comparison of Adverbs*.)

'Only' as an Adverb

'Only' deserves a section to itself. It is sometimes used as an adjective, as in 'You are my *only* hope' and 'an *only* child'; and sometimes as an adverb equivalent to *merely*.

As an adverb it is very versatile, since it is used to qualify each part of speech (except, of course, nouns and pronouns); and for this reason its position in a sentence can be important. I am speaking here particularly about written English, where there is no emphasis or tone of voice to make the meaning clear. In the sentence 'I caught sight of John on Monday', the addition of the word 'only' can have several results, according to where it is placed:

1. '*Only* I caught sight. . .' This means that I was the only person who saw him and that my friends did not see him. *Only* is an adjective in this sentence. In the other examples it is used as an adverb.
2. 'I *only* caught sight of. . .' This suggests that I merely saw him in the distance, but was unable to speak to him.
3. 'I caught sight *only* of John. . .' Here the implication is that I didn't see anyone else.
4. 'I caught sight of John *only* on Monday (or on Monday *only*).' But I didn't see him on another day of the week.

It seems that the one safe position for *only* is in front of the word or phrase which it qualifies, except at the end of a sentence as in four, where it may also follow its word or phrase.

The Comparison of Adverbs

Like adjectives (Chapter 6), adverbs have three degrees of comparison: positive, comparative and superlative. As we have seen, many adverbs are formed by adding *-ly* to the adjective; these adverbs, like many adjectives, use *more* and *most* to form their comparatives and superlatives. For example:

Positive	*Comparative*	*Superlative*
beautifully	more beautifully	most beautifully

Some words, however, are used in the same form both as adverbs and adjectives in each of the three degrees of comparison. For example, *early*:

1. *Positive*: 'The *early* bird catches the worm' (adjective); 'This train leaves *early*' (adverb).
2. *Comparative*: 'I shall catch an *earlier* train tomorrow' (adjective); 'It leaves *earlier* in the morning' (adverb).
3. *Superlative*: 'The *earliest* train leaves at one a.m.' (adjective); 'And it arrives *earliest* of all' (adverb).

A few well-known adverbs have unexpected forms for their comparatives and superlatives, usually the same forms as their related adjectives. For example:

Positive		Comparative	Superlative
well	(adjective *good*)	better	best
badly	(adjective *bad*)	worse	worst
*little	(adjective *little*)	less	least
*much	(adjective *much*)	more	most

*These two adverbs, like *early* above, are exactly the same as their related adjectives in all three columns.

Sentences III

Adverbs perform two functions:
1. They qualify individual words or phrases.
2. They qualify the main verb of a sentence, so that the whole meaning of the predicate is affected.

1. At the beginning of this chapter we saw that adverbs can qualify five parts of speech. Here are some illustrations of this:

Qualifying an adjective: The road is *perfectly* straight.

Qualifying another adverb: The time passed *very* quickly.

Qualifying a conjunction: I shall tell you *exactly* how I did it.

Qualifying a preposition: She arrived *just* before five o'clock.

Qualifying a verb: To travel *hopefully* is better than to arrive.

Each of these adverbs qualifies a single word (*straight, quickly, how, before, travel*). As we have already noticed, a phrase may do the work of a one-word part of speech. In this case the phrase may be qualified by an adverb. For example:

They went abroad *for a holiday*. (Adverb phrase)
They went abroad *merely* for a holiday. (The adverb *merely* qualifies the adverb phrase.)

2. The most important function of an adverb is to qualify the main verb of a sentence. This affects not only the meaning of a single word but the meaning of the whole predicate.

Here are the sentences that were used at the end of Chapter 7 in *Sentences II* to illustrate various kinds of predicate:

We enjoy ice cream.
She told her sister this story.
Birds sing.
The sky was blue.

All of these predicates may be qualified, and often enriched, by the addition of adverbs or adverb phrases:

We *tremendously* (How) enjoy ice cream *at the seaside* (Where).
She told her sister this story *quietly* (How) *after tea* (When).
Birds sing *sweetly* (How) *for joy* (Why) *in the spring* (When).
The sky was *always* (When) blue *in Italy* (Where).

The words in brackets point out what kind of qualification the adverbs and adverbial phrases add to the original predicates.

We must also notice here the important little adverb *not*, which would have the effect of reversing the meaning of any of these sentences. Other negative adverbs include *never* and *nowhere*. For example:

We do *not* enjoy ice cream. Birds *never* sing. *Nowhere* was the sky blue.

We are now able to express in tabular form the structure of a simple sentence, using the four sentences to which we have added adverbial qualifications:

Structure of Simple Sentences

SUBJECT	PREDICATE				
	Verb	Direct Object	Indirect Object	Complement	Adverbial Qualifications
We	enjoy	ice cream			tremendously at the seaside
She	told	this story	her sister		quietly after tea
Birds	sing				sweetly, for joy, in the spring
The sky	was			blue	always, in Italy

Notice that we have needed a separate column for the adverbial qualifications of the main verb, because they affect the meaning of the whole predicate. On the other hand, in the sentence 'The sky was *very* blue', the added adverb *very* belongs to its adjective blue and so is part of the complement.

The expression in tabular form of the component parts of a sentence is called *analysis*, a term familiar in scientific and other fields. The analysis of more complicated sentences will be found in Chapter 18.

Summary of Adverbs
1. Adverbs qualify any parts of speech except nouns, pronouns and interjections.
2. Especially they qualify verbs, as their name suggests.
3. The main kinds of adverbs are:

   a) Adverbs of place
   b) Adverbs of time
   c) Adverbs of manner
   d) Adverbs of reason and purpose
   e) Interrogative adverbs
   f) Conjunctive adverbs

4. There are also sections on everyday adverbs which require careful identification; on adverbs according to usage; on the word *only*; and on the comparison of adverbs.
5. Adverbs perform *two functions*: first they qualify individual words or phrases; and second they qualify the main verb of a sentence, so that the whole meaning of the predicate is affected. The adverbial qualification of the predicate is explained in the last section of the chapter, and is illustrated by the analysis of four sentences (*Sentences III*).

14

Conjunctions

Definition

The word 'conjunction' means 'joining together'. Conjunctions are used to join *words* ('cat *and* mouse') and *sentences* ('We admire him *because* he is kind').

Conjunctions Joining Words

The conjunctions used for this are *and, but, or* and *nor. And* may be preceded by *both. Or* is sometimes paired with *either* and *nor* is usually paired with *neither*.

So in a weather forecast, for example, we may join the two adjectives 'cold' and 'fine' in four ways, each with a different meaning according to the conjunction used:

1. The weather will be (*both*) cold *and* fine tomorrow.
2. The weather will be cold *but* fine tomorrow.
3. The weather will be (*either*) cold *or* fine tomorrow.
4. The weather will be *neither* cold *nor* fine tomorrow.

Conjunctions Joining Sentences

Sentences joined together to become parts of one larger sentence are called *clauses*, as we have already discovered in Chapter 5 (see *Relative Clauses*) and in Chapter 11 (see *Conditional Clauses* and *The Subjunctive in Other Subordinate Clauses*).

The conjunctions that join clauses include those that join words (see above). These conjunctions join words of equal importance (cold *and* fine) and clauses of equal importance. For example:

We shall buy that book *and* you may borrow it.

We shall buy that book *or* we shall borrow it from you.

Relative pronouns and relative adverbs *sometimes* perform the same function as *and* in joining equally important clauses. For example: We met the author of that book, *who* (= *and* he) greatly impressed us. We found the book in an old bookshop, *where* (= *and* there) we also found other books by him.

The two clauses of equal importance in each of these sentences are called *co-ordinate clauses*.

Most conjunctions, however, attach dependent or *subordinate clauses* to a main clause. We shall return to the distinction between co-ordinate and subordinate clauses in Chapter 17. Meanwhile, here are some of the conjunctions introducing subordinate clauses:

Relative pronouns: who, which, that:
> The book *that* you gave me for Christmas was fascinating.

Relative adverbs: where, when:
> The dictionary *where* I found this word is out of print.
> Do you know the year *when* it was published?

Conjunctions of place: where, wherever:
> We shall buy it, *where* (or *wherever*) we see it displayed.

Conjunctions of time: when, after, before, while, since, until:
> *When* I have finished the book, you may borrow it.
> *Since* it was first published, it has been issued as a paperback.

Conjunctions of reason: because, since:
> *Since* I am not enjoying the story, I shall not finish it.

Conjunctions of purpose: that, lest; *and the phrases* so that, in order that:
> See examples in Chapter 11 of subjunctive clauses expressing purpose.

Conjunction introducing a result: that; often preceded by *so* or *such*:
> I found the book so interesting *that* I recommend it to everybody.

Conjunctions introducing conditions: if, supposing, whether. . .or:

We shall buy that book, *if* we see it in a bookshop.

We shall buy that book, *whether* you recommend it *or* not.

Conjunctions introducing concessions: though, although:

We shall buy that book, *though* (or *although*) it has an unattractive cover.

Conjunctions introducing clauses giving a report of what is said and thought:

Your brother said *that* you came home yesterday.

We thought *that* you would arrive on Monday.

Your friends have been asking *how* you are travelling.

The other interrogative adverbs (see Chapter 13) can also be used in this way.

To conclude this chapter about conjunctions, here are a few *comments and cautions*:

1. You will notice that in most cases the two clauses used in these sentences are reversible. '*If* we see it in a bookshop, we shall buy that book' conveys exactly the same meaning as it does the other way round. Conjunctions belong to the clauses which follow them, so here *if* has moved with its clause to the beginning of the sentence.

2. Many of the words used in this chapter perform two functions at the same time. *Relative* pronouns and *relative* adverbs may equally well be termed *conjunctive* pronouns and adverbs, because they are pronouns and adverbs doing the work of conjunctions. Similarly, *where* and *wherever* are conjunctive adverbs of place; *when, after* and *before* are conjunctive adverbs of time; and the interrogative adverbs *where? when? how? why?* may introduce 'clauses giving a report' (see above) as conjunctive adverbs, *but without their question marks*.

3. Some of the words used as conjunctions in this chapter may be other parts of speech when they are used differently. For instance, *before* may be a

conjunction or a preposition or a simple adverb; *after* may be a conjunction or a preposition (see *Preposition or Adverb?* in Chapter 15). The word *that* has various uses as a conjunction (see above); it can also be a demonstrative pronoun or a demonstrative adjective.

4. *Than.* By a majority verdict the experts regard *than* as a conjunction but allow that it is sometimes quite properly used as a preposition. See *Than* in Chapter 15.

5. *Like* and *except* are not conjunctions but prepositions. The very colloquial 'Like I said' should be 'As I said'. *Except* was a conjunction in old English, but in modern speech we must say '*Unless* you do this' (not '*Except* you do this').

6. *And* and *but.* To begin a sentence with either of these words was once frowned upon. But this appears to be no longer so – see *The Complete Plain Words*, new edition 1987. However, too many *and*s and *but*s can become monotonous.

Summary of Conjunctions

1. Conjunctions may join words. The ones used for this purpose are *and, but, or* and *nor*.

2. These and other conjunctions are used to join clauses. There is a list of conjunctions joining co-ordinate clauses, and also a selection of the conjunctions introducing subordinate clauses. These are fully illustrated by examples.

3. Some comments and cautions about conjunctions include notes on conjunctive pronouns and adverbs, and on words which may be used either as conjunctions or as some other parts of speech. There are also comments on the words *than, like* and *except, and* and *but*.

15

Prepositions

Definition

Prepositions are words placed in front of nouns or pronouns, which are their objects; see the section on the accusative in Chapter 4.

Placed in front of their objects, prepositions produce phrases expressing ideas like place, time, manner (the way something happened), purpose and cause. This may sound familiar because these *word groups* of preposition-and-noun are often – though not always – equivalent to adverbs; in this case they are called *adverb phrases*. (See Chapter 13.)

Examples of Prepositions

Here is a list of the commonest English prepositions. The first ten have examples of objects attached to them.

Preposition	*Object Noun or Pronoun*
about	midday
above	the sky
across	the river
after	this
against	the enemy
along	the road
among	friends
around	the town
at	the cinema
behind	me

Other prepositions include: behind, before, beneath, beside, between, beyond, by, concerning, during, except, for, from, in, inside, like, near, of, off, on, opposite, over, past, through, to, towards, under, up, upon, with, within, without.

Note that *of* plus a noun or pronoun is a *genitive phrase*. Similarly, *to* and *for* plus a noun or pronoun are often (but not always) phrases equivalent to a *dative* case. This can be particularly important in other languages. See the sections on the genitive and the dative in Chapter 4.

Preposition or Adverb?

Many of the words in the list above live a double life: they can be either prepositions or adverbs (or, occasionally, some other part of speech). Their part of speech in a particular sentence depends on the old test: how is the word being used? One of the following three definitions will fit most cases:

1. When the words have object nouns (or pronouns) they are *prepositions*, as in 'I told you that *before* tea.'
2. When they do not have object nouns (or pronouns) they are *adverbs*, as in 'I told you that *before*.'
3. *After* and *before* can play a third rôle: when they start a clause they are *conjunctions*, as in 'You heard that *after* (or *before*) you arrived' (see Chapter 14).

Preposition Phrases

Sometimes, instead of a one-word preposition, a group of words (a phrase) performs the same function. Examples include: '*according to* your story'; '*because of* this information'; '*owing to* the bad weather'.

Due to is another phrase of this kind which is now frequently spoken and written. *Due* in fact is an adjective which is correctly used in a sentence like 'His success is *due* to his efforts.' The use of *due to* as a preposition – as in '*Due to* his efforts he succeeded' – is still avoided by many people, though it does now appear in the dictionaries.

Where to Put Prepositions?

This may seem a strange question, since by definition a preposition is a word placed in front of its object. In English, however, though not in other languages, a preposition is frequently placed neatly at the end of a clause or sentence instead of in front of its object. This happens especially in relative clauses. For example:

1. The book *from* which I quoted was 'Julius Caesar'.

Here the preposition is in front of its object *which*. The clause may be reworded in one of the following ways with the preposition at the end of its clause:

2. The book which I quoted *from* was 'Julius Caesar'.
3. The book that I quoted *from* was 'Julius Caesar'.
4. The book I quoted *from* was 'Julius Caesar'.

At one time an artificial rule was taught in schools: 'Never end a sentence with a preposition.' This, of course, could lead to absurdities of the kind ridiculed by the suggestion that 'This is something I will not put up with' should be rewritten 'This is something up with which I will not put.'

In fact, good English usage allows us to put a preposition either in front of its object or at the end of its clause/sentence. But the result must always be clear and must never sound ugly or awkward.

I have only one piece of advice to add, and this is for students of languages other than English. Wherever a preposition may go in English, in other languages its place is in front of its object. So make sure you can recognize the object of a preposition.

Prepositions with More Than One Object

Prepositions can have more than one object, as in '*between* the reader and the author'; and '*with* my father or my mother'. If the objects are pronouns, rather than nouns, it is important to give them all the correct *object-forms*, or cases. For example: 'between *you* and *me*' (not *I*, a common mistake); 'with *him* or *her*'.

'Than': Preposition or Conjunction?

Here are two forms of the same sentence, using *than* in different ways:

1. She is cleverer than he (is).
2. She is cleverer than him.

The first form uses *than* as a conjunction joining two clauses; the second as a preposition followed by an object in the accusative case. There is no doubt that either of these is acceptable English. Some writers and most dictionaries regard the first option as more correct, but it undoubtedly sounds rather stilted unless we include the word *is*.

In some sentences, however, *than* must be treated as a conjunction if the meaning is to be clear. For example:

3. He likes her much more *than his brother does*.

In this sentence the verb in the *than*-clause is not optional, as it was in example one. If the verb is omitted, the meaning of the sentence is ambiguous; it may now mean 'He likes her much more than *he likes* his brother'. So, when in doubt, the safe rule is to treat *than* as a conjunction and supply a verb after it.

There is also one instance in which *than* must be recognized and treated as a preposition. This is when it stands before a relative or interrogative pronoun. For example:

4. I have been encouraged by my brother, than whom no one could be kinder.

Here, *than whom* (never *than who*) is always correct.

Finally, treat *than* as a possible trouble spot in a sentence. The important question is always whether or not the meaning is clear. If not, what I have said above may help you to understand why and to reshape the sentence.

Summary of Prepositions
1. Prepositions are usually placed in front of nouns or pronouns, which are their objects.
2. Some words may be prepositions or other parts of speech according to how they are used.
3. In English, prepositions may sometimes be placed at the end of sentences or clauses instead of in front of their objects.
4. *Than* may be used as a preposition or as a conjunction, but care is needed to avoid ambiguity.

16

Interjections

Definition

Interjections, the last of the eight parts of speech which were introduced in Chapter 1, are exclamations.

Their name derives from two Latin words: *inter* meaning 'among' or 'between'; and *-jection* from a verb which means 'to throw'. Interjections are words (or phrases or even short sentences) which are 'thrown among' the other words we speak or write. Here are a few examples:

Dear me! You are in a bad state.
Oh hell! I've hit my thumb again.
There, there! Don't cry, little one.
Whew! That was a close shave.

You can see that these interjections, unlike other parts of speech, have no *grammatical* relationship with other words. They are not subjects or objects or complements in a sentence, nor are they adjectives or adverbs qualifying other words. For this reason and also because many interjections are noises rather than intelligible words, some writers do not regard them as a genuine part of speech.

Notice that these and other interjections can be differently used: they may be made part of a sentence as, for instance, a subject or object:

'*Good Heavens*!' was his reply to everything we said.
He said '*Oh hell*!' whenever he hit his thumb.
These are no longer being used as genuine interjections but as equivalent to nouns. This becomes clear if the noun *nothing* replaces 'Oh hell!' in the second example: 'He said *nothing* whenever he hit his thumb.'

Interjections Without Words

Many interjections are merely noises through which we express joy, sorrow, surprise, anger, fear, disgust, pain and so on. In other words, their basic use is to express our feelings.

Some of these interjections are so common that they have crept into dictionaries as words in their own right. Examples include: *Oh!*; *Pooh!*; *Whew!*; *Er*; *Hem!* and *Hm*; *Tut! Tut!*; and *Sh!*

Interjections Using Words

Many words and groups of words are used as interjections. Examples include: *There, there*; *Look!* and *Look here!*; *Good gracious!*; *Good heavens!*; *Bless my soul!*; *Good-Oh!*

New interjections are coined every day.

Interjections in Writing

Since interjections have no grammatical relationship with the words around them, punctuation is used to separate them from their context in written English. The punctuation varies from the tame comma for the tame interjection ('This book, *alas*, is out of print') to the exclamation mark, which is the natural way of indicating an interjection: '*Hell!* I've missed my train. *What bad luck!*'

Summary of Interjections

1. An interjection is a word or group of words 'thrown among' the other words of a sentence without being grammatically related to them.
2. Many interjections are noises rather than intelligible words, and their basic meaning is to express our feelings.
3. Words used as interjections.
4. The punctuation of interjections.

17

Sentences, Phrases and Clauses

In the previous chapters we have concentrated largely on the individual parts of speech, the words which make up the English language. But words are not isolated units; we express out meaning through *groups* of words called sentences, phrases and clauses. These three word-groups have already been frequently mentioned, because we have found that we cannot adequately explain any particular word without noticing how it is used with other words, what function it is performing as part of a group. This chapter is designed to provide a fuller explanation of the three word-groups, sentences, phrases and clauses.

Simple Sentences

The structure of a *simple* sentence has already been studied in the final sections of Chapter 4 (*Sentences I*), Chapter 7 (*Sentences II*) and Chapter 13 (*Sentences III*). At this stage you will find it helpful to reread these three sections. *Simple* describes a sentence which has a single finite verb in its predicate. Here is a selection of the simple sentences that illustrated these earlier sections:

1. She told her sister this story quietly after tea.
2. Birds sing.
3. The sky was always blue in Italy.
4. Have you heard the birds singing?
5. What wonderful stories the old soldier told!
6. Listen carefully!

The structure of these sentences (the way their words are related to one another) is made clear by their analysis in tabular form. For the term analysis, refer to *Sentences III* in Chapter 13.

Tabular Analysis of Simple Sentences

SUBJECT	PREDICATE				
	Verb	Direct Object	Indirect Object	Complement	Adverbial Qualifications
1. She	told	this story	her sister		quietly after tea
2. Birds	sing				
3. The sky	was			blue	always, in Italy
4. you	Have heard	the birds singing			
5. the old soldier	told	What wonderful stories			
6. (you)	Listen				carefully

The analysis of sentences one, two and three appeared in Chapter 13 and is reprinted here for the reader's convenience.

Sentences four, five and six were explained in Chapter 4 (*Sentences I*). They are arrangements of simple sentences in the forms of a question, an exclamation and a command respectively. Remember that in a command the subject *you* is generally omitted in modern English.

We can see the structure of any simple sentence by analysing it in tabular form. The only parts which 'do not show up in analysis' are vocatives (Chapter 4) and interjections (Chapter 16), neither of which has a grammatical relationship with the other words in a sentence. For example:

'*Friends, Romans, countrymen*, lend me your ears.'
Oh hell! I've hit my thumb again.

We cannot show in tabular form either the vocatives (*Friends, Romans, countrymen*') or the interjection (*Oh hell!*).

The Work of Phrases and Clauses

Each of these word-groups is an *expanded form of one or other of the parts of speech* that we have studied in the previous chapters. So, for example, a noun phrase and a noun clause are both groups of words doing the work of a noun in a sentence.

Sentences containing phrases and clauses appear more complicated than the sentences we have been studying in the first part of this chapter, but it is important (and helpful) to remember that their structure is exactly the same.

Phrases in Sentences

A phrase is a group of words which does *not* contain a subject and its finite verb.

Some phrases contain a non-finite part of a verb, such as an infinitive, gerund or participle; many consist of preposition-plus-object. Phrases may do the work of nouns, adjectives, adverbs, prepositions and conjunctions, as the following examples will show:

Noun Phrases

As subject of sentence:
Where to find a house was greatly worrying us both.
As direct object of verb:
He told me *how to reach my destination*.
As complement:
His hobby is *constructing model railways*.
To enlarge another noun:
The question *what to do next* is our immediate problem.
(A noun or noun-phrase which is attached to another noun to enlarge its meaning is said to be *in apposition* to the first noun. Familiar examples include Edward *the Confessor*, William *the Conqueror*.)

Adjective Phrases

Like adjectives they describe, qualify or limit nouns (see Chapter 6). Here are two examples:
The track *across the mountains* is dangerous.
Our journey *to school* takes us through the town centre.
The phrases describe the nouns 'track' and 'journey'. They are practically equivalent to the single adjectives in 'The *mountain* track' and 'Our *school* journey'.

Adverb Phrases

Many adverb phrases were introduced in Chapter 13 on adverbs, where you will find two that were repeated earlier in this chapter in the illustrations of simple sentences (*after tea*, *in Italy*). Adverbs and adverb phrases may qualify a number of parts of speech (see Chapter 13), but here we are concerned with adverb phrases qualifying the finite verb of a sentence and so affecting the meaning of the whole predicate. Here are two examples, each containing two adverb phrases:

We travelled *across the mountains at day break*.

The bus takes pupils *to school every day*.

The four adverb phrases qualify the verbs of their sentences, telling us where and when the action takes place. Notice, incidentally, how two identical phrases, *across the mountains* and *to school*, have been used to perform different functions, as adjectives in the last section and here as adverbs.

Finally, here is a type of adverb phrase that contains a noun and a participle (verbal adjective) qualifying it. For example:

The clock having struck four, I made the tea.

My book finished (or *being* or *having been finished*), I went to bed.

These phrases tell us when the actions of the main verbs of the sentences (*made* and *went*) happened. In some English grammars and foreign language textbooks you may find them called *absolute* phrases.

Preposition Phrases

These have already appeared in Chapter 15 on prepositions. They are worth mentioning only because they do the work of prepositions in forming many adjective and adverb phrases.

Conjunction Phrases

Here is an example:

Owing to the fact that it was raining, he cancelled his appointment.

This long phrase is equivalent to the conjunction *because*, here introducing the clause *it was raining*. Other conjunction phrases include *in order that, so that, in case*. More about the work of conjunctions and conjunction phrases in sentences will be found in Chapter 14 on conjunctions and in the next section of the present chapter.

Clauses in Sentences

Sentences that are joined together to become parts of one larger sentence are called its clauses; the joining words are called conjunctions (Chapter 14). Unlike a phrase, therefore, a clause is a group of words that *contains a subject and its finite verb.*

Clauses may be of equal rank or order in a sentence, in which case they are known as *co-ordinate* clauses; alternatively, one may be the *main* (or principal) clause and the other(s) its *subordinate* (or dependent) clause(s).

A sentence consisting of two or more co-ordinate clauses is called a *compound* sentence.

A sentence containing a main clause (or clauses) and one or more subordinate clauses is called a *complex* sentence.

Co-ordinate Clauses

These are joined by the conjunctions *and, but, or, nor*. They relate events in the order in which they happen, each clause continuing or adding to what has already been said. For example:

We shall buy that book *and* you may borrow it.

In conversation, a string of simple sentences like these are often joined together as co-ordinate clauses of one large sentence:

We shall buy that book *and* you may borrow it, *but* you must return it *or* we shall not lend you the sequel *and* then you'll be sorry.

You can see by reading this why too many co-ordinate clauses should be avoided in writing English.

Sometimes co-ordinate clauses share a subject. For example:

We bought that book *and* then (we) lent it to you.

Relative pronouns and relative adverbs may join co-ordinate clauses when they are equivalent to *and.* . . as we saw in Chapter 14. Here are two examples used in that chapter:

We met the author of that book, *who* (= *and he*) greatly impressed us. We found the book in an old bookshop, *where* (= *and there*) we also found other books by him.

We shall find that we need to distinguish these clauses from *subordinate* clauses beginning with the same pronouns and adverbs. As you read the following sections on subordinate clauses, study the uses of *who, which, that, where, when*; and see also below *Relative Clauses of Two Types.*

If we wish to analyse a sentence containing co-ordinate clauses, we treat each clause as a separate simple sentence, omitting for this purpose the conjunctions *and, but, or, nor.* But relative pronouns and relative adverbs must appear in analysis, and the simple sentences in the last two examples are:

We met the author of that book // who (= he) greatly impressed us.

We found the book in an old bookshop // we also found other books by him where (= there).

Subordinate Clauses

Subordinate clauses in sentences are *dependent* on the *main* (or principal) clause and so they are not equal partners but of lower rank (*sub*ordinate).

Subordinate clauses are expanded forms of three parts of speech; they *do the work of nouns, adjectives and adverbs.*

Noun Clauses Do the Work of Nouns

As subject of a sentence:

Why he acted like this is still uncertain.

As direct object of a verb (a very common use):

He reported *that you had arrived.* He asked her every year *whether she would marry him.*

As complement:

A victory at Twickenham was *what every player hoped for.*

In apposition (for this term see *noun phrases* above):

The news *that victory had been won* was received with joy. (In apposition to subject.)

We heard the news *that victory had been won.* (In apposition to object.)

It was obvious *that everybody had miscalculated.* (The clause is in apposition not to a noun but to the subject pronoun *it.*)

As object of preposition:

They were delighted by *what had happened.*

You have seen from these examples that noun clauses may be introduced by *that, why, whether* and *what.* Also frequently employed are the words we first met as interrogative pronouns and adjectives (*who, whom, which*) and as interrogative adverbs (*where, when, how,* in addition to *why* already mentioned). We must not, however, be tempted to give them question marks; they are talking about questions but not actually asking questions (see the first noun-clause example above).

Remember that the correct case of *who* and *whom* is decided, as in relative clauses, by their function *in their own clauses.* For example:

I do not know / *who* did it. (Nominative, subject of *did*)

I do not know / *whom* you expected. (Accusative, object of *expected*)

Adjective Clauses Do the Work of Adjectives

This means that they *qualify* or *limit* nouns and pronouns (Chapter 6). Subordinate adjective clauses are always closely attached to their own nouns and pronouns, and so *not separated from them even by commas.* They are relative clauses (see Chapter 5 on pronouns) introduced by relative pronouns or by the relative adverbs *when* and *where.* The subordinate clauses are similar in appearance to the co-ordinate relative clauses earlier in this chapter, but they have a different function; the distinction between the two is examined below in the section *Relative Clauses of Two Types.* Meanwhile, here are some examples of subordinate adjective clauses used to describe nouns:

The man *who has a beard* is my grandfather. (= The *bearded* man is my grandfather.)

I cannot remember the place *where I was born.* (= . . .my birthplace.)

The book *that you gave me for Christmas* was fascinating.

The dictionary *where I found this word* is out of print.

Adverb Clauses Do the Work of Adverbs

You will remember from Chapter 13 that the most important function of an adverb is to qualify the main verb in its sentence. This is the function of adverb clauses: they tell us where, when, how, why (reason or purpose), with what result, under what conditions (including concessions) the action of a main verb takes place.

The use of conjunctions to introduce adverb clauses was illustrated in Chapter 14, and most of the sentences that follow are reprinted from that chapter. Notice that adverb clauses, unlike noun and adjective clauses, can generally be placed before or after their main clauses without affecting the meaning of their sentences.

1. Adverb clause of place (where):
   We shall buy it *where* (or *wherever*) *we see it displayed.*
2. Adverb clause of time (when):
   When I have finished the book, you may borrow it.
   Since it was first published, it has been issued as a paperback.
3. Adverb clause of manner (how):
   I speak *as I find.*
4. Adverb clause of reason (why):
   Since (or *because*) *I am not enjoying this story,* I shall not finish it.
5. Adverb clause of purpose (the aim or intention):
   She is telling her story *in order that everyone may know the facts.*
6. Adverb clause of result:
   I found the book so interesting *that I recommend it to everybody.*
7. Adverb clause of condition:
   We shall buy that book *if we see it in a bookshop.*
8. Adverb clause of concession:
   We shall buy that book *though it has an unattractive cover.*

Relative Clauses of Two Types

In this chapter I have pointed out two types of relative clauses: one type is a subordinate adjective clause, the other is a co-ordinate main clause. The two perform different functions and, in written English particularly, it is important to use them correctly; otherwise, we may not say what we mean. In what follows, the figures 1 and 2 denote the first type and the second type.

Consider these two sentences, each containing a relative clause:

1. London trains *that depart from platform five* arrive on time.
2. London trains, *which depart from platform five*, arrive on time.

Apart from the change of relative pronoun (more about this later) and the addition of commas, the second sentence is often regarded as interchangeable with the first. But the commas make a clear distinction, as we shall see, by showing how the second relative clause is to be read and spoken.

1. London trains *that depart from platform five* arrive on time. The relative clause in this sentence is an adjective clause, which like an ordinary adjective is not separated from its noun by a comma. The clause performs the function of an adjective by limiting the meaning of its noun (see the definition of the function of an adjective at the beginning of Chapter 6); here it joins another adjective (*London*) in limiting the noun *trains*. So the effect of the clauses is to limit the London trains the sentence is talking about to the ones departing from platform five, as distinct from (say) the ones from platform six or seven. This meaning becomes even clearer if we replace the adjective clause with an adjective phrase:

London trains *departing from platform five*. . .

or even:

Platform-five London trains. . .

Here are some further examples of adjective clauses limiting the meanings of their nouns:

The club disciplined all its players *that (who) were guilty of foul play*. (Here the clause has the important function of limiting the disciplined players to the guilty ones.)

The shoe *(that) the old woman lived in* was too small for her family.

The house *where we spent the night* belongs to my sister.

The time *when the train arrives* is important.

Summary: Relative clauses of the adjective type must not be separated from their nouns even by a comma; the whole group of words, noun with its adjective clause, is read or spoken without a pause.

The function of these clauses is to limit their nouns. They begin with the relative pronouns, *who* (whom, whose), *which, that,* but they often prefer *that.* The relative pronoun is frequently omitted altogether when it is an object; for instance, 'The shoe that the old woman lived in. . .' ('The shoe *in which* the old woman lived. . .') becomes 'The shoe the old woman lived in. . .'

The relative adverbs, *where* and *when,* may also begin adjective clauses.

2. London trains, *which depart from platform five,* arrive on time.

The relative clause in this sentence is separated from the rest of the sentence by pauses, marked by commas. This has the same effect as would be produced by placing brackets round the clause; the clause is adding another equally important fact and is really a *co-ordinate main statement.*

The two equal statements made by this sentence are: London trains arrive on time. London trains depart from platform five. Compare this with what has been said about sentence 1.

A relative clause of this kind often follows the other clause in the sentence and the comma may then be regarded as meaning *and. . .*

This makes it easy to see that the relative word is adding a new fact or event concerning its antecedent:

The club disciplined all its players, *who were guilty of foul play.*

This means:

> The club disciplined all its players *and* they were (all) guilty of foul play.

(The clause adds a further fact about all the players.)

Sometimes the statement of the relative clause is a comment on what the first clause has said:

> The flight was five hours late, *which (and this) caused hardship to travellers.*

The relative adverbs *where* and *when* may begin clauses of this type:

> At last we reached my sister's house, *where (and there) we were warmly welcomed.*

Summary: Relative clauses of the co-ordinate type are always isolated by commas (or comma and final full stop when they end sentences); often brackets provide a good alternative punctuation, especially in the middle of sentences. The punctuation is important because it is intended to show the reader that a further fact, event or comment is being added to an already-complete statement. The clauses begin with the relative pronouns *who* (whom, whose) and *which* (but not *that*) and the relative adverbs *where* and *when*; the relative word is never omitted.

Summary of Sentences, Phrases and Clauses

1. A *simple* sentence is a group of words containing a subject and its finite verb. The finite verb agrees with its subject in person and number.
2. A phrase is a group of words which does not contain a subject with its own finite verb. Phrases are used as expanded forms of several parts of speech. The most important are noun phrases, adjective phrases and adverb phrases.
3. Clauses are sentences which have been joined together by conjunctions to become parts of a larger sentence.
4. Co-ordinate clauses are clauses of equal rank in a sentence. A sentence consisting of two or more co-ordinate sentences is called *compound*.

5. Subordinate clauses are of lower rank and dependent upon the main clause in their sentence. Subordinate clauses are of three kinds, representing expanded versions of three parts of speech: noun clauses, adjective clauses and adverb clauses. A sentence containing a subordinate clause (or clauses) is called *complex*.

6. Relative clauses are of two kinds: subordinate adjective clauses, which limit the meaning of their nouns; and co-ordinate clauses, which add a further fact, event or comment to the sentence.

18

Analysis and Complex Sentences

Analysis is a technique for examining the structure of a sentence. Like other techniques, it requires some initial practice but once acquired it improves performance without our being conscious of using it. We certainly should not dream of analysing every sentence we write; that would be disastrous for creative writing. On the other hand, if we understand sentence-construction, we can often write more effectively and avoid saying what we do not intend.

The analysis of simple sentences has been studied in previous chapters (4, 7, 13, 17). This chapter will apply the technique to complex sentences. The first stage in analysing a complex sentence is to discover what clauses are used and what work they do in the sentence. The clauses may then be listed and the function of each indicated.

In the following passage the sentences are numbered for easy reference:

1. We *enclose* with our compliments the illustrated brochure you *requested*. 2. You *will see* that it *contains* a list of recommended hotels and also *indicates* where you *will find* English dishes on the menu. 3. *Should* you *require* any further information, your enquiry *will be welcomed* at our local office, which *is* open daily from 9 to 5.

All clauses must have *finite verbs*, and so we start by identifying and marking them; in the passage above they have been printed in italics.

The finite verbs lead us easily to their *subjects*: *We* (enclose), *you* (requested), *You* (will see), *it* (contains), *it* (indicates), *you* (will find), *you* (should require), *your enquiry* (will be welcomed), *which* (is). We have noticed that *it* is the subject of two verbs. We can now conclude that:

Sentence 1 has two clauses with no conjunction joining them, but the omission of a relative pronoun (*that*) is quickly diagnosed.

Sentence 2 has a *that*-clause with one subject (*it*) and two verbs (*contains, indicates*); it also has a clause beginning with the conjunctive adverb *where*, leaving *You will see* as the main clause.

Sentence 3 begins with a conditional clause with the conjunction *if* idiomatically omitted (see *Conditional Clauses* in Chapter 11). The next clause must be the main clause 'answering' the condition. The *which*-clause is a relative one and the comma preceding it tells us which type it is.

We are now able to tabulate the clauses in these sentences and to describe their functions:

Clause/Function Table

CLAUSE	FUNCTION
Sentence 1	
(a) We enclose with our compliments the illustrated brochure	MAIN CLAUSE
(b) (that) you requested	Subordinate adjective clause limiting *brochure* in main clause
Sentence 2	
(a) You will see	MAIN CLAUSE
(b) that it contains a list of recommended hotels (and)	Subordinate noun clause, object of *see* in main clause
(c) (that it) also indicates	Ditto
(d) where you will find English dishes on the menu	Subordinate noun clause, object of *indicates* in clause (c)
Sentence 3	
(a) Should you (*if* you should) require any further information	Subordinate adverb clause of condition, qualifying *will be welcomed* in main clause
(b) your enquiry will be welcomed at our local office,	MAIN CLAUSE
(c) which is open daily from 9 to 5	Relative clause of co-ordinate type adding another MAIN statement (see last chapter)

Notice that in Sentence 2 the last noun clause (d) is dependent on the previous noun clause (c); it is thus doubly subordinate.

If we need to do so, we can now analyse each of these clauses as a simple sentence. For this purpose, the relative pronouns and relative adverbs are needed since they do the work of pronouns or adverbs as well as conjunctions; the other conjunctions (*that, and* in Sentence 2) are merely connecting words joining clauses and may be disregarded in the analysis of the clauses themselves.

The tabular analysis that follows is arranged in the same way as the analysis of simple sentences in the previous chapter.

Tabular Analysis of Clauses

SUBJECT	PREDICATE			
	Verb	Direct Object	Complement	Adverbial Qualifications
1(a) We	enclose	the illustrated brochure		with our compliments
1(b) you	requested	(that)		
2(a) You	will see			
2(b) it	contains	a list of recommended hotels		
2(c) it	indicates			also
2(d) you	will find	English dishes on the menu		where (=there)
3(a) you	should require	any further information		
3(b) your enquiry	will be welcomed			at our local office
3(c) which (=it)	is		open	daily from 9 to 5

19

Capital Letters and Punctuation

Capital Letters
Capitals are used to begin words of the following kinds:

1. The first word of a sentence.
2. Proper names of people, places, months, days, etc – eg, James Watt, Leicester Square, Germany, Russia, Asia, February, Friday. Adjectives related to proper names also have capitals – eg, Russian roulette, Yorkshire pudding; but there is a tendency to regard some very common expressions as equally correct without capitals – eg, french (or French) polish, wellington (or Wellington) boots.
3. Courtesy titles used in addressing people or speaking about them, such as Mr, Mrs, Sir, Lord, the Right Honourable. 'Dear Sir' or 'Dear Madam' is used at the beginning of formal letters.
4. Titles of *particular* people – eg, Her Majesty the Queen, the President of the United States, a Justice of the Peace.
5. Names of religious bodies and festivals – eg, the Church of England, Jehovah's Witnesses, Easter, the Passover, Ramadan, Holi.
6. Titles of books, plays, films, newspapers, etc – eg, *The Importance of Being Earnest*. As a general rule, only the first and important words of a title are capitalized, which in practice means that prepositions, conjunctions and articles, unless they are at the start of the title, usually begin with lower-case (small) letters.

7. The start of a quotation, often after a comma or colon. For example:
   > He replied with another question, 'What evidence have you for this?'

   But notice what happens in the middle of a quotation:
   > 'You have no evidence,' he replied, 'to support your statement.'

8. The personal pronoun I always has a capital letter; so often have the old O of the vocative and the exclamation Oh!

9. Until quite recently, the first word of each line of a poem was invariably capitalized:
   > Oh, to be in England
   > Now that April's there. . . (R. Browning)

   Modern poets do not always follow this practice.

10. Abbreviations using initial letters for names or titles – eg, USAF (United States Air Force), BMA (British Medical Association), BA (Bachelor of Arts). Such abbreviations were once written with full stops (B.A.), but in modern usage the omission of the full stops is equally correct.

I have included in this list most of the present uses of the capital letter in English. The student will know that the 'rules' in a foreign language are not necessarily the same; for instance, the Italians use a lower-case letter for the names of months and days of the week. Every language has its own conventions.

Punctuation Points

History and Purpose of Punctuation

A system of punctuation by the use of points or dots is said to have been invented in the third century BC in the city of Alexandria. It was a city of scholars and students, which possessed the most famous library in the ancient world. The *aim* of the invention was a thoroughly practical one: it was intended to be an aid to readers of the great Greek authors such as Homer, a very necessary aid at a time when manuscripts were written continuously, with no divisions between words or sentences.

The system was later adopted and developed by the Romans and their successors. In the Middle Ages it was called punctuating or 'marking the points', from the Latin word *punctum*, a point. (Hence the French *point*, the Spanish and Italian *punto* and the German *Punkt*.)

Modern punctuation is more sophisticated than the Alexandrian system, but its aim is unchanged: it is intended to help the reader. A writer employs it to show his readers how he wishes them to read what he writes; which words are to be read as a group; when his words are in the form of a question or an exclamation rather than a statement; when to pause and when to stop. Without any punctuation, even a short sentence can be misinterpreted, as in the following roadside notice seen by a reader of the *Daily Telegraph*:

GOOD FOOD ALL DAY LEFT UNDER BRIDGE

In the following notes about various punctuation marks, I shall try to distinguish essential from optional uses in current practice.

Full Stop (also called Period)
All sentences end in full stops (a question mark or an exclamation mark is equivalent to a full stop where appropriate). On the other hand, it is not correct to end any other word-group with a full stop, as happens in the following:
'At last we reached our destination. An old half-tim-bered house in the country.'
The second group of words has no finite verb; it is a phrase not a sentence. The remedy is to put a comma after destination, replacing the full stop, and so produce a single sentence:
'At last we reached our destination, an old. . .'
Alternatively, if two short sentences are required, we can write:
'At last we reached our destination. It was an old. . .'
Full stops are considered optional in abbreviations consisting of initial letters (see *Capital Letters* 10, above). Abbreviations using the first and last letters of words do

not have full stops – eg, Dr, Mr, Bp (Bishop). Many full stops in other abbreviations are fast becoming optional – eg, p.o. or po for postal order; Nov. or Nov for November; i.e. or ie for 'that is' (from the Latin *id est*); etc. or etc (for the Latin *et cetera*) meaning 'and the rest', 'and so on'.

Question Mark

The question mark, one of the two possible substitutes for the full stop at the end of a sentence, is only used to ask a question (Where are you going?), never to report or talk about a question (I asked where you were going).

Exclamation Mark

The exclamation mark, the other possible substitute for the full stop, follows words or phrases used as interjections (see Chapter 16). It is also sometimes appropriate with a short command that is close to being an exclamation – eg, 'Come here at once!' A whole sentence may also be exclamatory – eg, 'What a wonderful time we had on your birthday!' In our personal letters to friends we probably use exclamation marks to mean something like 'Just imagine that' in sentences like 'They didn't arrive home until well after midnight!!!' This is a practice to avoid in serious writing.

Apostrophe

The possessive or genitive form of nouns has an apostrophe (see *Genitive Case* in Chapter 4), but not so the genitive forms of certain pronouns (yours, his, hers, its, ours, theirs, whose; see the sections on *Personal* and *Relative Pronouns* in Chapter 5). Otherwise, apostrophes show that letters are omitted: it's (it is), don't (do not), shan't (shall not).

The apostrophe in the possessive case of a noun does in fact represent the omission of the letter *e* in the old English form of the genitive case. In *The Canterbury Tales* Chaucer speaks of 'the *kynges* court' (the King's court).

Quotation Marks (or Inverted Commas)

These have already been illustrated above, in *Capital Letters* 7. They are used when someone's actual words are quoted.

The modern practice is to use single commas 'like this', except for a quotation inside a quotation:

The witness replied: 'The police constable stopped me and asked, "Do you realize, Sir, that you are driving without lights?"'

In the last sentence notice the position of the quotation marks. The witness's words are enclosed within single inverted commas; the police constable's question, including its question mark, are placed within double inverted commas. Hence the punctuation (?"') at the end of this sentence.

There are further illustrations of the correct position of quotation marks in *Chambers Pocket Guide to Good English* under the entry *quotation marks*.

Comma

The comma (like the colon and the semi-colon) is a punctuation mark *inside a sentence*, between the capital letter at the beginning and the full stop at the end.

Some commas are considered essential and some are optional. A writer will use the optional ones for emphasis or clarity; in the examples below these will be placed in brackets (,).

Sections 1–10 below illustrate many of the commas that are generally regarded as essential in good writing today, together with a few now treated as optional.

1. Lists of three or more items, people or actions. Note the *and* before the last word in each list:

She arranged her pen, pencil, ruler(,) and calculator on her desk. We got up, washed, dressed, had a quick breakfast(,) and ran to the station.

This pupil works enthusiastically, neatly(,) and intelligently.

There is an optional comma before *and* in each of these sentences. Notice, however, that the comma is essential before the *and* introducing the last item in:

Shakespeare's plays include *The Tempest, The Merchant of Venice, Julius Caesar, Romeo and Juliet*, and *Antony and Cleopatra*.

2. A series of adjectives before a noun may have the same punctuation as in 1 above:

A tall, ugly(,) and depressing building.

Or it may omit the *and* and keep the comma:

A tall, ugly, depressing building.

Sometimes the last adjective in a list belongs so closely to the noun as to produce a single idea, such as *government building, post-war building*. One of these expressions may replace the single word *building* without affecting the punctuation:

A tall, ugly(,) and depressing post-war building.

Apart from their uses in a list (1) and with a series of adjectives (2), commas should be regarded as brackets and therefore *go in pairs*. A frequent mistake is to write the first comma and then forget to 'close the bracket', so you should look for the second comma in each of the following sentences. (Of course no comma is used at the start of a sentence or at the very end.)

3. Vocatives require commas to avoid ambiguity:

Children, never treat animals cruelly.

Always telephone, *John*, before you come.

Jane is in the garden helping her, *mother*.

4. Absolute phrases (see *Adverb Phrases* in Chapter 17) are adverb phrases containing a noun and a participle. They are enclosed in commas:

The day's work being finished, he at last went home.

I think that, *all things being considered*, you acted wisely.

5. Other phrases containing participles are used to qualify the subject or object of a sentence. They are usually enclosed in commas:

Strolling out into the garden, he sat down in the sun.

The headmaster entered the hall and, *having stood for some minutes in silence*, he addressed the assembly.

In phrases like these the participles are a neat way of avoiding a string of finite verbs. They replace:

He strolled out into the garden *and* he sat down in the sun.

The headmaster *entered* the hall *and* he stood for some minutes in silence *and* he addressed the assembly.

Some participle phrases, however, are merely descriptive, especially when they follow their nouns or pronouns:

We watched the barrels *being rolled* into the warehouse.

She watched her children *sleeping* peacefully.

These phrases do not require commas.

6. Two or more adjectives immediately following their noun are usually enclosed in commas:

The river Weser, *deep and wide*,
Washes its wall on the southern side...
(R. Browning)

7. So is a group of words including a noun standing in apposition to another noun:

This valley, *now a beautiful sight*, was once a battlefield.

Dante, *Italy's greatest poet*, wrote *The Divine Comedy*.

The nouns *sight* and *poet*, each with its own qualifying words, are in apposition to *valley* and *Dante* respectively.

Notice, however, that no comma is used in expressions like 'William the Conqueror' and 'Alfred the Great'.

8. Between co-ordinate clauses:

The co-ordinating conjunctions are relative pronouns and relative adverbs together with *and*, *but* and *or*. When they introduce co-ordinate clauses, the relative words always require commas (see *Relative Clauses of Two Types* in Chapter 17). *And* is mostly not preceded by a comma; a comma before *but* and *or* is optional and may be used for contrast or emphasis.

9. Adverbs and adverb phrases:

Here the commas are optional:

Finally(,) he repeated the question(,) even more insistently.

However(,) *despite all his efforts*(,) he received no reply.

One-word adverbs like *finally, however, nevertheless, indeed* and others with more than one syllable are often given commas, particularly at the beginning of a sentence. Many writers would place a comma before the long adverb phrase *even more etc* and commas round *despite all etc*. This is a matter of individual taste and emphasis in each case; they are not essential commas.

10. Adverb clauses (see examples in Chapter 17):
An old rule once said that all adverb clauses, except very short ones, should be enclosed in commas. Sometimes this rule was modified to apply only to adverb clauses preceding the main clause. Present usage treats adverb clauses in the same way as adverbs and adverb phrases in 9 above. Whether or not to enclose an adverb clause in commas is left to the individual writer's judgement. The following examples show the same clause in different positions in three sentences:

If he comes at all(,) I hope to see him.
My attitude is that(,) *if he comes at all*(,) he will be welcome.
He will be welcome(,) *if he comes at all*.

Finally, here are a few examples of what are regarded as *Commas to be avoided*:

1. One comma when two are required. Commas are used *in pairs* in the examples in 3–10 above. See these sections and the remark preceding section 3.

2. A relative clause of the subordinate (adjective) type must not be separated from its noun by a comma. See *Relative Clauses of Two Types* in Chapter 17.

3. No comma should stand between a subject and its verb (except when a phrase itself requiring two commas is placed after the subject; see 6 and 7 above):

The vase you can see on the windowsill is the one I bought in Rome.

The complete subject ends at *windowsill*; no comma is required at this stage.

4. A noun-clause object should not be preceded by a comma:

> I cannot discover *what he is doing*.
> You told me *that you would come*.
> They gave instructions *that no one should be told*.

(Noun clauses italicized. See Chapter 17.)

5. A comma is not an adequate stop between two independent sentences; see *Full Stop* above. In what follows the comma is incorrect:

> I called on him in London, he was not at home.

(Use a full stop, a colon or semicolon, a conjunction [and, but], or a dash [see below]).

Semicolon and Colon

The *semicolon* is the halfway stop between a comma and a full stop. It can stand instead of a conjunction between clauses that could otherwise be separate sentences, especially when the clauses are linked in sense or contrasted:

> He had said his last word; the incident was finished.
> Jane was distressed; her friends were overjoyed.

Sometimes the second clause begins with a co-ordinating conjunction (and, but).

Semicolons may also punctuate lists of events or items, often after a first clause ending in a colon:

> They had brought with them all their equipment: tents and groundsheets to protect them from the weather; tins of food and drink (and a tin-opener); John's radio for entertainment (and for news, he said); and, on their mothers' orders, lots of warm clothing.

One use of the *colon*, to introduce a list, has just been illustrated. Another is to introduce direct speech as an alternative to a comma; (see above, *Capital Letters* 7). You will also have noticed in a book of this type how useful a colon is to indicate that an example follows.

Hyphen

A hyphen makes two or more words into one compound word, such as *tin-opener*. This is a stage in the never-ending process by which *tea pot* became *tea-pot* and finally *teapot*.

Clearly there can be no final rule about hyphenated words; we all refer to a dictionary when in doubt. For more information see *hyphen* in *Chambers Pocket Guide to Good English*.

Brackets

I have already mentioned that brackets and a pair of commas produce similar effects. Sometimes they can be substituted for commas without harming the 'flow' of a sentence:

Dante (Italy's greatest poet) wrote *The Divine Comedy*.

However they have a stronger isolating effect than commas and in many sentences they would not be suitable replacements.

A further use of brackets is to isolate a parenthesis:

If his train is late (which heaven forbid!) he will not arrive in time for his wedding.

A *parenthesis* is a brief comment or explanation or exclamation inserted in a sentence. It may take the form of an interjection, and like an interjection it has no grammatical connection with the rest of the sentence. The plural form parentheses sometimes means the brackets enclosing a parenthesis.

Dashes

1. A pair of dashes may be used exactly like a pair of brackets to isolate a parenthesis:

   If his train is late – which heaven forbid! – he will not arrive in time for his wedding.

   At the end of a sentence the second dash is replaced by a full stop (or question mark or exclamation mark):

   I know the guests have arrived and that the bride is in tears – but what can I do?

   The second dash is similarly omitted before a colon or semicolon.

2. This last example illustrates a common use of the dash: it can introduce a comment or further information about what has just been said.

3. A single dash is also used instead of a colon to introduce a list or a quotation (see *Colon* above). A

combination of the two (: –) was once common, but is now regarded as unnecessary.

4. In a long sentence the subject may continue for some time before the writer reaches his verb. Here a dash can mark the end of the subject (a comma should not be used here; see *Commas to be avoided* 3):

> Packing the possessions accumulated over three years here, taking tearful leave of so many friends, the frantic rush to the station, and then the apparently interminable journey to London – all this left her emotionally and physically exhausted.

You may not wish to write many sentences like this one, but you can see how effectively the dash marks the end of the list of events in the subject, which is then summed up in *all this* before the verb.

Summary

This chapter has dealt with:

1. Capital letters.
2. The history and purpose of punctuation.
3. Marks used in punctuation, including; full stop; question mark; exclamation mark; apostrophe; quotation marks; comma (essential and optional commas, commas to be avoided); semicolon and colon; hyphen; brackets; dashes.

Books for Reference

There is one indispensable reference book for all those who are interested in words: it is, of course, a good dictionary. The other books mentioned below form a personal selection from books I have found useful.

Dictionaries

I have made constant use of *Chambers Twentieth Century Dictionary* and *The Concise Oxford Dictionary*. There are other similar single-volume dictionaries, such as the *Collins English Dictionary* and *Webster's New International Dictionary*. You may already possess your own favourite. The later the edition the better: the English language is constantly acquiring new words, and old words add new meanings and usages while losing others.

Other Books

There are two classics of the grammatical genre—a little dated now, despite revisions, but still extremely good value; both contain a wide variety of alphabetically-arranged articles on grammatical topics and related subjects:

Fowler, H.W.: *Modern English Usage* (Oxford University Press; 2nd edition, revised by Sir Ernest Gowers, 1968)

Partridge, Eric: *Usage and Abusage* (Penguin Reference Books; revised edition 1973)

Here are three more recent books:

Davidson, G.W. (ed): *Chambers Pocket Guide to Good English* (Chambers, 1988). This is in the same series as the present book and contains entries on grammar, vocabulary, spelling, pronunciation and punctuation. The entries are conveniently arranged in alphabetical order.

Gowers, Sir Ernest: *The Complete Plain Words*, revised by Greenbaum and Whitcut (Penguin Reference Books, 1987). The author wrote this book (originally in two volumes) 'to help officials in their use of written English as a tool of their trade', but it quickly became popular with a much wider public. It has a good index, which is helpful when you wish to refer to a particular word or topic.

Carey, G.V.: *Mind the Stop* (Penguin Reference Books, reprinted 1976). Subtitled 'A Brief Guide to Punctuation', this is an interesting and entertaining book for those who wish to study the subject further. Eric Partridge called it 'the best short book' (on punctuation). This book too has a useful index.

Index

CAPITAL letters indicate chapter-headings and some major topics. Main page-references are printed in **bold** type.